Science
and Religion:
The re-opening
Dialogue

Science
and Religion:
The re-opening
Dialogue

edited by Gerald Walters

Bath University Press
1970

✝

Gerald Ivan Walters
1st May, 1970

215
8416

72-1952

EDITORIAL NOTE

The following papers are substantially as they were presented to a Conference of Anglican and Methodist clergy, held in the Centre for Adult Studies, Bath University of Technology, on 6th and 7th May, 1969. Members of the Science and Religion Group of the Centre for Scientific and Technological Affairs, Bath University, also participated in the Conference. The sermon presented in the Appendix was given by Canon Geoffrey Paul, Director of Clergy Training for the Diocese of Bristol, at the Conference service, held in Bath Abbey, 6th May, 1969. The Summary of Seminar Group Reports was edited from tape recordings.

CONTRIBUTORS

Anthony Barnard — is Vice-Principal, the *Theological College, Wells*.

R. A. Buchanan — is Senior Lecturer in Social History, and Director of the Centre for the Study of the History of Technology, *Bath University of Technology*.

David Edge — is Director of the Science Studies Unit, *University of Edinburgh*.

Gerald Walters — was Reader & Head of Humanities, and Director of the Centre for Scientific and Technological Affairs, *Bath University of Technology*.

Contents

Science and the Recovery of Being

Gerald Walters

'Since the seventeenth century, the activities of the human spirit have been strictly classified in separate compartments. But, in my view, the attempt to eliminate such distinctions, by a combination of rational understanding and mystical experience of unity, obeys the explicit and implicit imperative of our contemporary age.' (W. Pauli.)[1]

Any discussion in depth of issues in science and religion must begin with a consideration of the dominant cognitive attitudes effected by the development of the empirical sciences since the seventeenth century—and, important for the possibility of any resumption of 'dialogue' between the two, an assessment of the contemporary reaction in scientific thinking against the reductionism of the dogmatic and over-simple empiricism which has, down to the present, driven a fundamental division between 'being and knowing'. As Gellner puts it,[2] a scientific society is one in which 'the whole balance between *being* and *knowing* the ecology of existence and cognition, has undergone fundamental changes'. It is vital to understand the nature of these changes and the contemporary attempt to reassert the unity of being from within the sciences themselves. As the manifesto of the recently formed Study Group on the Foundations of Cultural Unity emphasises[3] there have been broad counter-movements, attempts to restore metaphysics and to reformulate a unitary concept of knowledge—in particular, existentialism and phenomenology. 'Movements of this sort have been strongholds, defying the current scientific movement, but they do not appear to be equipped for over-throwing and replacing it.' Effective counter

[1]

revolution, it is rightly argued, can only come from within the sciences themselves and this, it should be added, only when it becomes abundantly clear that empirical reductionism does not only invalidate the metaphysical and the mytho-poetic, moral, and aesthetic modes, which are seen as anomalies to be removed by further scientific progress, but also endangers the practice of science itself. It is with this counter-revolution within the sciences that this paper is primarily concerned.

The distinguishing feature of the culture of advanced scientific and technological societies from the seventeenth century down to the present, as Pauli[1] rightly insists, has been fragmentation and differentiation, the compartmentalising of bodies of knowledge and a sharp dichotomy between the knower and the known. Indeed, as the history of science clearly demonstrates, the phenomenal growth of science has so far derived precisely from this proliferation of specialist disciplines and techniques. The accumulation of minutiae of knowledge within the limitations of accepted paradigms is a natural and necessary part of the processes of what Kuhn[4] calls normal science. Intellectual differentation is itself sociologically institution-alised in the growth of occupational specialisation—reaching perhaps its ultimate refinement in the 40,000 recognised occupational groups in the United States, and requiring the development of formal bureau-cratic organisations of varying degrees of complexity to impose a limited and functional unity in technological and industrial processes. Above all, it has been a culture with a unique degree of intellectual compartmentalisation, not merely in the sense of a multiplicity of disciplines incapable of communication outside themselves, but one which, in a much more profound and psychologically disturbing way, has bifurcated the human being by separating him in his traditionally human concerns, including religious experience, from the cognitive processes of, at any rate, the mechanistic interpretation of science and technology which has been dominant until the present.

As Oppenheimer put it in his famous Columbia address,[5] itself a remarkable confession of faith of a man and a scientist only too deeply conscious of the dangers of a dichotomised culture, the frontiers of science are separated now by specialised techniques, vocabularies, arts and knowledge from the common heritage of even a most civilised society. The result has been the progressive reduction of the traditional leaders of culture, the writers, the poets, the artists, the musicians, the mystics, the philosophers, to the margins of culture. There has indeed been a major *crisis in the humanities*,[6] involving its practitioners in an increasing sense of irrelevancy. The writer, the artist and, we would add, the theologian must indeed, as Oppenheimer insists, at the end of his work communicate with an audience that must be men and not a specialised set of experts, bringing in intimacy directness and depth an intelligible interpretation of life. But where, he asks, is this community of men? Largely not there; the traditions, the history, the myths and the common experience which it is his function to illuminate, to harmonise and portray have dissolved in a changing world.

This has certainly been true of the epoch dominated by the reduction of Newtonian cosmology and Cartesian logic, as Marjorie Grene describes it, to 'a science of inorganic nature—bits of matter qualified by mass, spatial relations and the change of such relations',[7] the bare realities out of which a universe was constructed with mathematical exactitude and experimental ingenuity, and extended in to human affairs in pursuit of an exact science of man and society based on the automatic manipulation of unambiguous objective variables. In the last analysis this Newtonian-Cartesian universe is indeed a 'world without life'[6] driving a logical division between its form of knowledge and lived experience. It is important perhaps to qualify this by recalling the original achievement of the Newtonian-Cartesian system as providing a conceptual framework within which the 'new science' could develop without a catastrophic dislocation of the traditional European cultural pattern. The new methodology of the empirical sciences may have destroyed the *a priorism* of medieval scholasticism, but a universe written as Galileo described it, in mathematical characters still retained law and did not preclude faith. The human body and its physiological system could be described in mathematical terms as *res extensa* but mind and human consciousness remained of a different order, not derived from matter and not reducible to it. As Marjorie Grene puts it,[8] the acceptance of Newtonian mechanics involves an act of faith; and if Descartes had to invoke God *ex machina* to hold together mind and matter, he was still sufficient of an unquestioning Augustian for the invocation to work. It was the increasing secularisation of thought which rendered the synthesis untenable, over the last century in particular, to the point where all nature, human and animate as well as non-organic came to be envisaged in terms of the mechanistic laws governing their least parts—a new form of particulate ontology.

The experimental mode has persisted, however—and strongly enough to provide the basis for a revolution in thought—the demand

[3]

by human beings for *verstehen*, for understanding against the calculi of the logical machine, for personal involvement and commitment over and against the logical structures which separate the conscious mind from that which it seeks to understand or control, the subject against the non-personal object, for wholeness and completeness against the fragments. Whilst it may be argued that the reaction against the Newtonian-Cartesian universe follows a major shift of scientific interest away from the so called dead sciences to the disciplines which are concerned with life,[7] in particular the biological sciences—away from what Pantin calls the 'restricted' to the 'unrestricted' sciences—this is to over-simplify and to underrate the changes of outlook which are taking place. This is indeed the threshold of a philosophical revolution as profound as that which took place in the seventeenth century with the growth of the empirical sciences, arising as much in the context of the *dead* sciences as in the *life* sciences. It is not without significance that the leaders of the contemporary revolution in physics kept alive their own psychic roots in the mythopoetic world of the imagination—Oppenheimer with sixteenth and seventeenth century French poetry, Heisenburg with Goethe and Plato's *Timaeus*, Teller with the poetry of Ady.[9] Did not Oppenheimer rightly envy children playing in the street who still retained those lost modes of perception without which some of his most complex problems could not be solved?

The present intellectual revolution springs directly from the desire for a cognitive wholeness and completeness, and manifests itself on several levels of experience. It is in part a cultural revulsion against the excessive fragmentation of knowledge, a demand for a synthesis which can only be achieved at a high level of conceptualisation which embraces and resolves apparent dichotomies, complexification being succeeded by unanimisation as a Teilhard de Chardin would describe the process. This is indeed the ideal which Jaspers sets the contemporary university, of a truly comprehensive awareness of our age in the terms of the sum total of its knowledge, its practice and skill, the awareness of the wholeness and oneness of all knowledge[10]— an ideal which, however, imperfectly is implicitly recognised in the changes in organisation and curricula which have marked most postwar university development in Britain.

It is, further, a demand which does not arise solely at a theoretical level. The necessity of what Lindsay called *combined seeing* lies inherent in the nature of a continually advancing scientific and technological community, both in its fundamental lines of enquiry and in the way in which it formulates and seeks to resolve its problems. As research becomes increasingly problem centred rather than discipline centred where is the line of demarcation to be drawn, in the social sciences for example, between sociology, psychology, economics or history—or, in the biological sciences, between chemistry, physics or biology itself? The norm becomes that of the *multi-disciplinary* research team rather than the group of specialists, especially in the consideration of a whole range of problems which are social in origin and therefore multidimensional. The nature of the enquiry itself imposes a working unity on what have come to be regarded as disparate disciplines. This is of course, far removed from the comprehensive synthesis say of an Aquinas—indeed it might be doubted whether a philosophical exercise of this type, derived from extrinsic rather than intrinsic concepts is necessary or desirable. What is important is that at the point of application in society, knowledge which has been pursued and acquired in isolation is recalled to a fundamental unity; society provides its own organising concept.

But it is a revolution which involves far more than the interrelatedness of knowledge, important as this is, and going far deeper than the attempt to develop synthetic philosophies which are intrinsic to the methods of the sciences.

What is sought is a scientific universe derived from the world as experienced and lived, and an understanding of the process of scientific thinking which does not draw a sharp distinction between itself and other primary modes of experience, between reason and imagination, between the logic of the sciences and the logic of the mytho-poetic. Earlier theories of scientific method combined mechanistic Baconian inductionist logic with equally mechanistic linear stimulus-response models of learning. Discovery was presented as the final sequence of a mechanical chain of reasoning, proceeding from the patient collection of facts unprejudiced by theory—defined by Pearson as the classification of facts and the formulation of judgment upon the basis of this classification.[11] The philosophy of logical positivism was the *ultima ratio* of this approach to the methodology of science: all propositions which were not derived from empirical data and subject to the same principles of verification as the sciences were to be rigorously excluded. Statements of a theological, aesthetic, or metaphysical nature were epistemological 'nonsense', there was one cognitive system only. Attempts were made, notably by Russell, and the positivists of the Wiener-Kreis, to create

[5]

a new language freed from traditional symbolism, which would express more perfectly an isomorphic relationship between knower and fact. Scientific thinking was to be maintained in isolation from the other modes of experience which found their expression traditionally in art, music, poetry, literature, myth and liturgy. The experienced world as Marcuse emphasises[12] comes to be derived from 'restricted experience', and the 'explosive historical dimension of meaning' is silenced in the one-dimensional language of reductionist science.

The reaction against this view of the way scientific thinking proceeds, does not, it must be emphasised spring from an obscurantist wish that this were not the scientific method, a psychological yearning for a lost Eden. It derives from the more subtle contemporary understanding of the complex psychology of thought, and in particular of the processes of innovation and discovery in science —processes which are in no way distinct from creativity in the arts. The truth is that no scientist ever worked in this way. As Medawar says[13] induction has the rather discouraging property that it is not actually used by anybody, except in rather specialised senses by mathematicians and electrical engineers—'people speak of induction, they write about induction, but they do not actually use it.' Even when a Darwin maintains that he has worked on true Baconian principles and without any theory, collected facts on a wholesale scale, his private note-books and letters show that the opposite was in fact the case. It is this radical change of emphasis which has in effect produced the contemporary philosophical revolution. Whether initially conceived as phenomenological, existential or pragmatist, and despite differences of emphasis, the result has been to reawaken, as Merleau-Ponty expresses it, this primary experience of the world from which science is derived.[14] As Waddington insists, all experience is a unity, which cannot be analysed, as science necessarily must do, without in some sense violating it.[8] Scientific activity cannot be divorced from a metaphysical sense of this unity, this sense of the whole which subsumes the parts.

There are, in human experience, no isolated units of sense-data which are later, after due process of logical reasoning, organised into a schema; in fact is never a pure fact. Nor is order in experience a given *a priori*, a category, an idea in God's mind, a universe of Platonic ideas. The organising of experience is a subtle process interrelating knower and known. Order is continually made out of disorder by our ability to give meaning to our experiences. We do

[6]

not give meaning to our experience from any position of transcendence, but in a sense discover meanings, by responding to solicitations already in our experience. We organise the world from within experience, what Heidegger calls 'being-in-the-world'. The significant reality is the human reality, with its intentional structuring of experience, the *world-for-me* which is central to Merleau-Ponty's philosophy of phenomenology. The act of observation cannot divide observer and observed, whether in art or quantum physics. Nor is it possible to draw a distinction between the fundamental processes of scientific or artistic creation. Whether expressed in the terms of Cassirer as *radical metaphor*,[15] or of Koestler as *bisociative thought*[16] or of Schon as the *displacement of concepts*,[17] creative thought emerges as the intuitive bridging of areas of experience previously unconnected, what Einstein called a kind of combinatorial play.[15] Nor is this a mechanical process from which emotion and commitment are absent. On the contrary emotion plays as large a part in the production of a scientific hypothesis as in the creation of a work of art, that experience of the *magnum mysterium* which was to an Einstein 'our primitive perception of profoundest reason and most radiant beauty'[18] or to a Frank a feeling of terror analogous to a mystic's experiences of the noumenal.[19] Nor in this context, for all the misinterpretation of his ideas, both by the logical-empiricists and logical positivists, must the essential mysticism of Wittgenstein and its importance in his understanding of the nature of science, be overlooked.[19]

Indeed Polanyi's own analysis[20] of the stages of scientific thought can be applied with very little shift of emphasis to any form of creative work. Whether the act is called *intuition* or the *tacit co-efficient* of a scientific theory by which it bears on experience, the creation of a new hypothesis begins with a leap of the imagination. 'Every interpretation of nature is based on some intuitive concept of the nature of things', and discovery rests upon the interplay of intuition and observation, the discerning of *gestalten* that are aspects of reality. The process involves a high degree of personal judgment and decision in which the rules of the so called method are applied as rules of art. The role of observation is simply to supply clues for the apprehension of reality—the apprehension of reality thus gained forms in its turn a clue to future observations, that is, the process underlying verification. The process has its characteristic rhythms, but most nearly, in Polanyi's view, resembles the 'creation of a work of art which is firmly guided by a fundamental vision of the final whole, even though that whole can be definitely conceived only in terms of its yet undiscovered particular'. Foreknowledge of the final whole, however unparticularised, guides conjecture with reasonable probability. The Baconian prescription for empirical research is a travesty of the real processes by which discovery is made.

Scientific activity is brought then to an existential unity with the traditional forms of human understanding—not, it must be stressed, to an identity, but as having its common origins in the desire to elicit meaningful structures out of its own areas of experience and guided by a common creative imagination. As Oppenheimer concludes,[5] both science and the arts belong to the *village*—his own symbol of the intimate, creative existence in contrast to the *highway*, that is, meaningless, mechanised society. They form 'communities of artists and scientists bound in freedom and co-operation by the common bond of humanity'. Both have a responsibility to assert the meaningfulness of existence against lack of meaning. Both the man of science and the man of art live always at the edge of mystery, surrounded by it. 'Both, as the measure of their creation have always had to do with the harmonisation of what is new with what is familiar, with the balance between novelty and synthesis, with the struggle to make perpetual order in total chaos.' Science and art, share a common obligation to 'keep our minds open and to keep them deep, to keep our sense of beauty and our ability to make it, and our occasional ability to see it in places remote, strange and unfamiliar'. Not an easy task in a 'great open, windy world—a rugged time of it', no doubt, but now as complementary and no longer antagonistic modes of experience. It is only necessary to extend the concept of the artistic to include religious and mystical experience, to see the importance of these changes of emphasis in weltanshaung of the natural sciences for the future of religion.

In the social sciences, the processes which are already far advanced in the natural sciences, can be said to be only at the beginning. Indeed in his perceptive examination of the dichotomy in contemporary culture, T. F. Torrance[21] finds it paradoxically in its most acute form in the split between the pure sciences and the social sciences. This is not the familiar and indeed rather superficial Snow thesis of a science—arts cultural polarisation, but rather the failure of the social sciences to keep abreast of the revolution in thought of the pure sciences. It would seem to be the case, Torrance asserts, that 'while the pure sciences, for the most part, have overcome the

Newtonian dualism between space and matter, and have broken free from rigid mechanistic concepts deriving from it, the social sciences are still deeply infected with dualist and instrumentalist notions of science, and have yet to develop within their own fields the kind of connection that comes to view in field theory'. The social sciences have as yet failed to resolve the Weberian paradox of explanation and understanding, *begreifen* and *verstehen*, at a time when the natural sciences have themselves begun to rediscover the unity between knowledge and experience.

It was perhaps inevitable that sociology for example, in its attempt to distinguish itself as a discipline from more traditional and subjective approaches like philosophy towards questions about the nature of human society, should develop strong methodical affinities with the empirical sciences, and to turn to the dominant physical sciences in particular for its characteristic paradigms. It cannot be denied that the development of statistical techniques, operational attitudes, and mathematical models, have given to the relatively new social sciences the means of making statements of a high degree of definition and precision, together with the methodological testing of hypotheses. The question of how far can social phenomena be reduced to mathematical description, even of great complexity is, however, being posed with a growing urgency. If as Pantin[22] argues the distinction in the sciences is to be drawn between the 'restricted' and 'unrestricted sciences', with only the restricted sciences, like physics reducible to mathematical models, how much further removed is social phenomena from the possibility of logico-mathematical analysis? Is it really possible to explain changes in dependent variables by causative changes in independent variables.[23] Can one really claim to measure so-called 'single variables' which are themselves highly complex phenomena? How can one presuppose the relative continuities of the physical sciences in any analysis of social happenings whose nature is essentially discrete? Does the concept of casuality stand up to a rigorous examination in the social context as the relation between belief and action.[24] How far are purely deductive propositions like Arrow's General Possibility Theorem, with its clear distinction in mathematical logic between 'the will of all' and 'the general will', applicable in social situations which can never fulfill the necessary conditions and contingent assumptions?[25] Even when the mathematical logic has been verbalised, how far are conceptual schemes, like the 'analytical abstractions' of Parsons which consciously draw on Marshallian

B

economic models, meaningful descriptions of complex interacting events in human society?

The unhappy result of undue emphasis on theories of science which are no longer tenable in the natural sciences themselves, has been, particularly in Britain, a sociology with an inability to formulate creative hypotheses, marked as the report of the Tavistock Institute to the Heyworth Committee expressed it[26] by 'both too much formal conceptualising of a shallow kind, and too much secondary manipulation of meagre primary data'. It is a sociology characterised by a tendency towards the reification of concepts, particularly restricting in a science in which there is not as yet a large corpus of tested knowledge, and by an even stronger tendency to reductionism, the uncritical and often naïve pressing of particularly psychological data into the conceptual mould. Nor are its linguistic problems, to be divorced from its conceptual apparatus. Questions of 'sociologese' involve more than linguistic analysis, as Runciman has demonstrated[27], but relate far more significantly to the nature and scope of sociological enquiry. It may well be true that if sociological generalisations are found to be valid or illuminating, then these are quickly absorbed into the vocabulary of more established disciplines, and that the residue remain part of sociological discourse as the aggregate of unsucccessful or provisional attempt to talk more precisely about collective behaviour. The tendency to over-elaboration of concepts however, a neo-scholasticism much in need of a contemporary Ockham's razor—derives more fundamentally from the attempt to create a specialised language which corresponds more closely to scientific-mathematical models, the ideal which defeated the positivists of the Wiener Kreis. Conversely it is highly significant that the most illuminating concepts such as 'alienation' have in fact been drawn from other than empirical sociology. Nor can it be said that the overall representation of society as, in Aron's phase[28], 'a type of *commedia dell'arte* in which the actors have the right to improvise along prescribed lines' has the quality of authenticity. Small wonder that Dahrendorf's[29] Herr Schmidt fails to recognise himself in '*homo sociologicus*', that 'role playing shadow' inhabiting a world of societal abstraction.

As Merleau-Ponty[30] has emphasised in the context of the social sciences, there is a 'myth of scientific knowledge which expects that from the mere notation of facts there should arise not only a science of worldly things, but in addition a sociology of knowledge, itself understood in an empirical manner, a knowledge having to constitute

[10]

a closed universe of facts, and inserting therein everything down to the ideas we invent to interpret them, and to get rid of so to speak, of ourselves'. Empirical sociology has been all too readily a victim of this myth, which it cannot be too strongly emphasised, is no longer held in the empirical sciences. 'Under the collective name of science', Merleau-Ponty continues, 'there is nothing but systematic arrangement, a methodological exercise narrower or wider, more or less meaningful, of that same experience which begins with our first perception'. Science buys its exactitude at the price of a schematisation. What then is to be done? The remedy, urges Merleau-Ponty, is to 'confront it with an integral experience'. Nowhere is this coming to be seen to be more urgent than in sociology. It has come to be recognised that there is an essential core of truth in Weber's retention of the distinction of the German Romantic between *Naturwissenschaft* and *Geisteswissenschaft*. To accept that there is a qualitative difference between natural phenomena and social phenomena is not to revert to earlier subjectivism. 'The "interior" to which it brings us', as Merleau-Ponty indicates, 'is not to a "private life" but to an intersubjectivity'. Societal phenomena is an intersubjective reality, which manifests itself in existential orientation both to 'normal' and 'crisis' situations. The search for *verstehen* is not to be understood as an act of empathy, extrinsic to the act of sociological analysis but as arising within the conceptual field of analysis. As Schutz[31] urges, 'the obervational field of the social scientist, namely the social reality, has a specific meaning and relevance structure for the human beings living, acting thinking therein'. The 'thought objects' constructed by the social scientists in order to grasp social reality must be founded upon the thought objects constructed by the common-sense thinking of men, living their daily life in the social world. Knowledge has to be grounded then in 'lived experience', otherwise as Winter has shown[32] abstract 'models of constituted identity of a society' are substituted for its 'projected meanings' which can only be found in the symbolic structures of society. The world is symbolically perceived, and not simply responded to physically. All culture patterns, Geertz reminds us[33] are systems or complexes of symbols, lying in the intersubjective world of common understandings, with sacred symbols in particular synthesising 'a people's ethos, the tone, character, quality of life, its moral aesthetic style and mood, and the world view, the picture of the way things in sheer actuality are, their most comprehensive ideas of order'.

What is implicit here is a major shift away from the attempt to

[11]

adduce mathematical models towards the eliciting of 'meanings' and 'noemata' in social phenomena. This is not to abandon rigorous methodological procedures, but the substitution of an existential for a mechanistic conceptual field. This recognition that the 'second order' constructs, which are the social sciences, must arise out of primary experience, has profound consequences for the 'sociological imagination' in liberating it from the tyranny of positivistic concepts. Social science needs as MacKenzie claims,[34] the creative idea, what Pareto dismissed as 'metaphysical poetry', to provide insights which enable us to see the vital elements in common between one social structure or situation and another, or even to ask the searching preliminary questions. This after all has been the characteristic of the founding sociologists of the 'grand tradition' who had, what Wright-Mills defined as the quality of the sociological imagination, the capacity to shift from one perspective to another.[35] If 'audacity and orginality'[36] and 'creativity and inventiveness'[37] are recognised as a necessary feature of a vital social science, then the need is for minds that are 'sensitised' by 'expressive' rather than 'instrumental'[38] contacts with religion, philosophy, literature, history the arts, and with the symbolic content of human existence. Analytical precision can only be attained with the realisation that it needs to be preceded and supplemented by methods which are different in kind. It is only in this way that Weber's paradox can be resolved, with the recognition that, as Dufrene[39] expresses it, 'there can be no rational science without existential knowledge ... but reciprocally, no existential knowledge without rational science'.

What, finally is the significance of these profound movements in scientific thinking away from crude empiricism towards 'the recovery of being'? Not, it must be emphasised, an occasion for premature syntheses; but rather the opportunity for the resumption of that dialogue which was assumed as natural in the early period of 'the new science' in the seventeenth century. The contemporary philosophy of dialogue, as Dubarle reminds us,[40] presupposes the possibility of 'human conversation where spiritual convictions confront each other', a 'confrontation of liberties'. Such a dialogue differs from dialogue undertaken in order to arrive at common insight into demonstrated truth, it is not 'reason-insight'. Rather it is a situation in which 'the action and thought of each of those taking part has to refer to a consciousness freely and differently established in its convictions'. It is not that truth is not sought in common, but it can only be sought indirectly through 'reason-liberty'.

This type of dialogue is indeed 'a common quest of liberty . . . a common effort to advance in the direction of more truth'.[40] The abandonment of a 'fundamentalist' position on the part of the sciences, opens the way for such a dialogue. The question which has now to be asked is how far the Christian church has itself sufficiently abandoned what MacKinnon calls 'the varying types of fundamentalism which stands in the way of the sort of renewal which the present not only demands but seems to make possible'.[41] How far is the church prepared to engage in genuine dialogue of equals.

To attempt a lengthy examination of the response of the church goes beyond the limits of this present paper. It is important however, to emphasise the clear signs that Christian thought and action is entering into a new and vital dialogic phase.[42] As Brauer expresses it, in the context of interdisciplinary studies in the Chicago Divinity School, 'one primary fact marks this new age—the pre-eminence of dialogue in all aspects of divinity', providing 'a new base, which will profoundly affect not only the systematic study of doctrines and beliefs, but the very dimension of religious studies'. Indeed the mark of vitality of contemporary religious studies is the extent of dialogue relationships with other disciplines, leading to a reshaping of the pattern of traditional theological curricula in the major theological schools. Theology so concerned becomes what van Buren has called 'a conversation with the changing culture of man'.[43] This does not mean that no place will remain for academic theology and traditional scholarship, but it is difficult not to agree with Marty that 'theology *versus Deum* so often seems to confront silence'.[44] A theology *coram deo* will necessarily engage in genuine dialogue, not only with the more obviously closely related disciplines of literature, behavioural and social sciences, but also with the natural sciences—believing, as Teilhard expresses it, at the same time, 'wholly in God and the World'. This is surely where the possibility of renewal lies—not in a retreat into an Eliadian form of cosmic primitivism, a return to the archaic, nor in an obsession with 'death of God' paradoxes of Christain atheism, but in creative dialogue at the frontiers of the new scientific disciplines. Bonhoeffer's famous question—'in what way are we in the *ecclesia*, not concerning ourselves as specially favoured, but as wholly belonging to the world'— finds its answer. No longer the duality of reason and imagination, of the empirical and the metaphysical, of science and religion—but identity in difference, complementary modes in the exploration of Being.

References:

1. W. Pauli, *Science and Western Thought*.
2. E. Gellner, *Thought and Change*.
3. M. Grene (ed.), *Anatomy of Knowledge*.
4. T. Kuhn, *The Structure of Scientific Revolutions*.
5. R. Oppenheimer, 'Man's Right to Knowledge' (Columbia address, 1954).
6. J. H. Plumb (ed.), *Crisis in the Humanities*.
7. M. Grene, *The Knower and the Known*.
8. in C. H. Waddington (ed.), *Towards a Theoretical Biology*.
9. R. Jungk, *Brighter than a Thousand Suns*.
10. K. Jaspers, *The Idea of the University*.
11. K. Pearson, *The Grammar of Science*.
12. H. Marcuse, *One Dimensional Man*.
13. P. Medawar, 'The Scientific Method', *The Listener*, 12 October 1967.
14. R. Merleau-Ponty, *The Phenomenology of Perception*.
15. E. Cassirer, *Essay on Man*.
16. A. Koestler, *The Act of Creation*.
17. D. A. Schon, *Displacement of Concepts*.
18. R. Michelmore, *Einstein*.
19. C. A. van Peursen, *Wittgenstein: Introduction to his Philosophy*.
20. M. Polanyi, *Science, Faith and Society*.
21. T. F. Torrance, *God and Rationality*.
22. C. F. A. Pantin, *The Relations between the Sciences*.
23. M. Lipton in *Guide to the Social Sciences*.
24. A. MacIntyre in *Philosophy, Politics and Society—II*.
25. W. G. Runciman, *Social Science and Political Theory*.
26. Tavistock House, Report to the Heyworth Committee.
27. W. G. Runciman, 'Sociologese', *Encounter*, December 1965.
28. R. Aron, *Progress and Disillusion*.
29. R. Dahrendorf, *Essays in Social Theory*.
30. R. Merleau-Ponty, *Philosophy and Society*.
31. A. Schutz, *Concept of Theory Formation in the Social Sciences*.
32. G. Winter, *Elements for a Social Ethic*.
33. G. Geertz, *Religion as Cultural System*.
34. M. MacKenzie, *Creativity in the Social Sciences*.
35. C. Wright-Mills, *The Sociological Imagination*.
36. T. W. Adorno, *On the Logic of the Social Sciences*.
37. P. Winch, *The Idea of a Social Science*.
38. R. Hoggart, *The Literary Imagination and the Study of Society* (Brit. Assoc., 1967).
39. M. Dufrene, *Existentialisme et Sociologie*.
40. D. Dubarle, 'Dialogue and its Philosophy', *Concurrence*, I, 1969.
41. D. MacKinnon, Gare Memorial Lecture, 1968 in *The Shipping of the Altars*.
42. see Gerald Walters, 'Secular Premise', in *Religion in a Technological Society*.
43. P. Homans (ed.), *The Dialogue between Theology and Psychology*.
44. D. Permar (ed.), *Frontline Theology*.

Science and Religion: An Analysis of Issues

David Edge

The topics which could justifiably be included under the heading of 'Issues in Science and Religion' are many, and each is in itself complex. In the past, 'issues' have arisen in such areas as the apparent conflict of the approaches, attitudes, norms and values of the separate communities of scientists and theologians; in the clash of implicit metaphysical systems or 'world-views'; in the relative emphasis laid in scientific and religious discourse on the 'literal' and 'metaphorical' use of language; and in the attempt of science, via the human and social sciences, to extend its purview so as to include religious experience and behaviour as subject matter—and, of course, quite apart from these more general issues, there have been a number of instances in which *particular* scientific findings have challenged conventional statements of religious belief. Many of these old conflicts are still alive, in various forms: prejudices, once formed, do not die quickly, and seem singularly resistant to reason. Like the habitual patterns of postures in a monkey colony, they lie beneath the level of self-awareness, and seem, indeed, to be designed especially to prevent us gaining an awareness that might be too painful.

In such a situation, progress can only be made by patient, detailed and open minded *analysis*.

The 'problems' may be more apparent than real, and they may be essentially insoluble: but, until they have been explored, who can say?

Incidentally, and very much in passing, I feel it worth pointing out that the scientific community, its behaviour, beliefs, language and stated purposes are just as open to the scrutiny of the human and social sciences as are religious phenomena, and the results are just as challenging to tired prejudice.

So what I have to say today will be tiresomely shortsighted and detailed: it will also be largely negative, since I want to suggest that one author who has approached these issues in the right manner is still guilty (albeit tentatively) of advancing a premature solution—worse, a solution of the wrong type, a response to a misunderstood problem.

The author is Ian Barbour, in his book on *Issues in Science and Religion*.[1] For the purposes of this paper, I take this book as read and so will make no attempt to repeat Barbour's admirable survey of the literature. I want to focus on what I take to be the crucial issues within Barbour's territory—which is itself strictly limited to the implications of natural science, and of the emerging picture of the structure and nature of matter in physical and biological form, to Christian theology. My major point is that the issue here is an unresolved problem in philosophical theology: namely, in what sense are religious assertions cognitive? Barbour's discussion of this point seems to me to be inadequate, and I want to argue that, as a result, his final conclusion is irrelevant.

I will group what I have to say under four loosely-related headings.

1. *Natural theology and a 'theology of nature'*

Barbour is not simply resurrecting Natural Theology: he is too sensitive to the insights of existentialism, and of linguistic analysis, for that. As he admits:

> Natural theology does not lead to the personal involvement and dependence on revelatory events which characterise the Western religious tradition (p. 237).

And he states his position early on, in these words:

> Though theology does indeed start from historical revelation and the realm of personal existence, it should not stop there. . . . The view we will propose is not a new 'natural theology' (that is, an argument for God from the evidence in nature), but rather a 'theology of nature', an attempt to view the natural order in the framework of theological ideas derived primarily from the interpretation of historical revelation and religious experience (p. 5).

Can this distinction between 'natural theology' and 'theology of nature' be maintained? We do not bring theological ideas to nature

[16]

in innocence: scrutiny of nature, even if only in an everyday sense, has given rise to at least some of these theological ideas in the first place. It is doubtful if we would have identified 'revelations of God' in history and experience, in the way we have done, if physical nature had been, as it were, invisible to us. Where do our metaphors of God's action and nature come from? Very often from the raging seas or the still calm that follows; from the destruction of earthquake and volcano, and the thrusting creativity of the spring. The metaphors feed our own conceptions of human, as well as of divine, potentiality, and conjure up a magic circle of images and associations, of attitudes both appropriate and inappropriate. The problem is one of *grounding* this seductive system. In what precise way does it *reflect* the character of the real world, and in what way *distort* it? In what way, perhaps, does it *create* it?

As John Wisdom in his famous essay on 'Gods',[2] points out, the attitudes and associations which accompany our perception of nature are embedded in our language—but they rest on 'unspoken connections', *carried* by the language but not *expressed* in it. To quote an example Wisdom himself uses, we continue to say 'the sun is sinking in the west', even though we no longer believe that the sun is 'actually' sinking. And so, in continuing to use the words, we may think ourselves merely indulging in a description: the sun 'looks as if it is sinking'. But are we really so detached from the lanaguge? Doesn't our continued use of this phrase also evoke a *mood*, an *attitude* which we would take to be an appropriate response to the scene, in a way that the phrase 'the earth has revolved so far that the sun's rays are now approaching a tangential path' does not? The different attitudes attendant on two verbal descriptions of this kind are, of course, 'subjective' inasmuch as they arise from the specific experiences with which we have, in the past, learned to relate the words used: but, as Wisdom argues, they have an 'objective' referent in that they are evoked by real features of the world, and these features may not be those consciously conserved in the change of description. They may be 'hidden', and a discussion of the appropriateness or otherwise of the attitudes involved may rest on the identification of these hidden features.

When, for instance, the scientist maintains that the material universe behaves in important respects like a clock, or the human brain like an electronic computer, he may think that his redescription limits itself to the specific respects he is considering. But it may well do more than to redescribe those aspects in a more useful and insightful way: it may also alter whole clusters of attitudes and dispositions in a way which, on inspection, proves to be *inappropriate* to *other* aspects which the scientist, in his analysis, has dismissed as irrelevant.[3] It is not always necessarily so, but it might be so, and the matter can be rationally debated.

This, Wisdom argues, is the case with the gods. Natural metaphors involve description *and* mood, and when, as is true in our language in so many subtle ways, they are the vehicle for our thought about persons and about ourselves, our perceptions and our attitudes may be incoherently muddled. Normally, we think that they can be separated: but, as Paul van Buren has said in a recent essay:[4]

> I find that the distinction 'cognitive/non-cognitive' is not helpful in getting clear about how Christian faith is a matter of how the world is, and I regret having once been seduced into picking up that stone axe as an appropriate tool for opening up this delicate bit of watch-works. The issue is not, as that distinction leads us to suspect, that we have an agreed frame of reference, an agreed way of carving up the world into tables and chairs on the one hand, and our attitudes or dispositions towards tables and chairs on the other. Christian faith, on the contrary, proposes another way to do the carving up in the first place.

It has, as I understand it, always been the aim of Christian metaphysics to propound fundamental categories which in themselves, hold together the descriptive and the dispositional. To maintain that the universe is a divine living organism, for instance, is both to *describe* its function *and* to mould our attitudes towards it. Wisdom does not propound any such metaphysics: but he does sketch out a method which hints at why such a metaphysics might be held to be necessary. In outline it runs as follows:

(*a*) By metaphorical transfer of natural symbols, and the incoherence of our perception of them and of our attitudes towards them, we can be trapped by forces within, of which we are from time to time dimly conscious—when we feel, as it were, 'taken over' by anger or lust which we are powerless to control. As he says:

> Now the gods, good and evil and mixed, have always been mysterious powers outside us rather than within. But they have also been within. It is not a modern theory but an old saying that in each of us a devil sleeps . . . Elijah found that God was not in the wind, nor in the thunder, but in a still small voice.

(*b*) Although we might not often be described as 'possessed', we are continually adopting, quite unconsciously, attitudes which others might challenge as inappropriate. (Wisdom quotes the example of the man tenderly lifting dying flowers, as if they 'felt'—although this behaviour might not be inappropriate to a butterfly.) The challenge involves drawing attention to these 'hidden' features. It is a matter of reasoning, albeit usually inconclusive.

(*c*) This process of reasoning will tend to weaken inappropriate aspects of our behaviour, but *it will tend to strengthen those which emerge as appropriate*. This, Wisdom refers to as 'a double and opposite-phased change'. Certain inner forces are then strengthened, and unified into some developing coherence: this development accompanies a *release* from a kind of dimly-apprehended inner trap. It therefore can be related to talk of salvation and redemption; and the whole process to talk of 'coming to know God'. Wisdom concludes his essay with these words:

> Many have tried to find ways of salvation. The reports they bring back are always incomplete and apt to mislead even when they are not in words but in music or paint. But they are by no means useless; and not the worst of them are those which speak of oneness with God. But in so far as we become one with Him He becomes one with us. St. John says he is in us as we love one another. This love, I suppose, is not benevolence but something that comes of the oneness with one another of which Christ spoke. Sometimes it momentarily gains strength. Hate and the Devil do too. And what is oneness without otherness?

(*d*) In the final stages of this process, perception and disposition will achieve a coherence which demands that the ultimate categories of the stuff of the universe follow suit. Mere tables and chairs will no longer suffice.

Now, I have embarked on this speculative introduction, partly because I want to allude to it later, but mainly at this juncture, because it expresses my doubts as to the validity of distinguishing a 'Theology of Nature' from 'Natural Theology'. If the process is as intimate as I have sketched out, no 'framework of theological ideas' can be 'derived primarily from the interpretation of historical revelation and religious experience'. At all points in both the springing of the trap, and the eventual release, the 'natural order' plays a direct role. It provides the literal base of many of the metaphors, and much of the evidence on which we can decide whether those metaphors are up to mischief.

We can now briefly state two fundamental problems of religious thought:

(a) Does this natural metaphorical trap contain built-in clues for the release? That is to say, are there natural symbols which, by the range and ambiguity of their associations, can maintain the kind of coherent unity-in-diversity required by our emergent 'knowledge of God'? Does the world (in Professor Hepburn's phrase) 'lend itself' to a reconciliation of this kind?

and

(b) Is the function of religious thought to attempt to encompass, and state in some way, the whole 'answer' to the 'riddle' thus posed —or is the riddle more like an Ximenes crossword, in which the most important insight is *what kind of a puzzle it is?* Does a theology try to 'give answers' or 'get people started'—or both? It is quite possible that the natural world 'lends itself' to the earlier stages of the puzzle, but that its symbolic resources are exhausted before the end.

2. *The cognitive function of religious assertions*

Barbour continually insists that it is not enough to maintain that religious language is merely 'inspirational', or that religious concepts are useful fictions'. For instance:

> The 'language of worship' includes assertions about what one worships. If people did not accept the truth-claims of religion, its varied 'uses' would disappear, for religious language is referential in intent. And in the absence of all cognitive elements, commitment would be arbitrary caprice (p. 248).

With this, I agree: the problem is to breathe some firm content into these phrases. For instance, Barbour comments:

> The man at worship, like the man in the laboratory, uses language with realistic intent, and yet he recognises that his symbols are not a replica of reality.

It is crucial here to clarify the meaning of the phrase 'realistic intent'. The goal of the religious quest may be 'realistic' (in the sense that its aim is a more satisfying engagement with the real world), and its language may be 'realistic' (in that it is an attempt to communicate the character of the ongoing experience of that quest), *without* the key images and symbols being *representational*, in the sense in which scientific theories are usually held to be an attempt to represent the nature of structural features of the physical world, and of its pattern of material flux. Two structures can be exhaustively defined in one frame of reference, without any hint of the kind of phenomenon which will emerge when the two are brought together. It is an essential property of a tightrope that it is capable of supporting an acrobat. But a description of an acrobat need not entail a description of a tightrope—nor (what is more to the point) a tightrope that of an acrobat. Indeed, some of the features of the tightrope which the acrobat exploits are just those which would deter any reasonable man from setting foot on it. In advance, we might well conclude that the performance is impossible (which is precisely why we pay good money to witness it). And yet we know that the acrobat can do it. He has demonstrated a possibility which, in a sense, 'flies in the face of the facts'. Perhaps religious truth exists in this kind of relationship to the world's 'structures'. The religious language, and its associated rituals, may be 'imaginative engineering': 'symbols of inner poise', you might say. They may have a sort of triangular relationship to the subject, on the one hand, and the world, on the other—expressing something discovered *in the dialogue between the two*. The phenomenon may be bounded by the structures, but not be translatable into (or deducible from) a description of either. The Way and the Life may not, after all, be contained in the Truth. Indeed, the plain implication of the Truth may be that both Way and Life are impossible—unless (as the acrobat does) we place undue emphasis on details that appear to be quite trivial, if not actually deterring.

Is this just a restatement of the inadequate view that religious concepts are 'useful fictions'? Perhaps it is. But it would not involve denying that they are, at least in some important senses, *realistic*, and related to facts.

However, the problem of cognition remains, and with it the crucial questions in the relationship between science and religion: in what way does theology regroup the facts of experience? And how does this regrouping relate (if at all) to the patterns which emerge from scientific analysis? Barbour just touches on this problem in a key passage of less than one page, which I will quote in full:

A first step toward granting *a limited cognitive function* to religious statements is evident in John Wisdom's famous essay, 'Gods'; he grants that religious statements are experimentally unverifiable, and yet holds that they have an objective reference and not a purely subjective one: their function is *to direct attention to patterns in the facts*. Religious language is not just emotive, for religious attitudes influence interpretations and suggest 'models with which "to get the hang of" the patterns in the flux of experience':

> It is possible to have before one's eyes all the items of a pattern and still miss the pattern . . . And if we say as we did at the beginning that when a difference as to the existence of a God is not one as to future happenings then it is not experimental and therefore not as to facts, we must not forthwith assume that there is no right and wrong about it, no rationality or irrationality, no appropriateness or inappropriateness, no procedure which tends to settle it, nor even that this procedure is in no sense a discovery of new facts. After all even in science this is not so.

Religious beliefs are not mere matters of feeling, since 'reasons for or against them may be offered'. Wisdom compares them with legal decisions in which the judge makes no simple logical deduction, yet his decisions are not arbitrary. Religious discourse involves drawing attention to connections, making analogies, comparing alternative interpretations, pointing out patterns, and portraying the features that fit the theistic model. Other authors have spoken of the realisation of a sense of contingency as 'a new way of seeing familiar facts', comparable to the sudden realisation of beauty in a landscape, or recognition that a pattern of lines on paper represents a three-dimensional cube. Such an 'attention-directing' function is related to empirical evidence, but no direct verification is expected (pp. 249–250).

Then Barbour leaves this issue, to discuss 'falsifiability', where 'evidence against' belief is couched in such terms as 'purposeless suffering'—terms which, as Barbour admits, require interpretation, and where the criteria of evaluation of the evidence derive, at least in part, from the beliefs they are meant to test. He does not return to Wisdom's argument.

And yet the one suggestion he offers as to the cognitive component of religious statements—'their function is to direct attention to patterns in the facts'—is a quite inadequate analysis of cognition, in either science or religion. 'Patterns in the facts' may exist, but have no significance, like faces in the fire. Barbour has already admitted as much in an earlier section on 'The Personal Judgment of the Scientist':

> Judgments as to what kinds of connections are plausible . . . influence one's interpretation of data. Consider 'Bode's Law', which correlates the radii of successive planetary orbits in the solar system with the succession of terms in a particular mathematical series. At one point scientists were impressed by the fact that agreement between the data and the formula was fairly good. Subsequently, when there seemed to be no conceivable explanation for such a law, the agreement was dismissed as a coincidence. But more recently there has been renewed interest in the significance of Bode's Law, in the light of new hypotheses concerning the origin of the solar system (pp. 179–180).

The 'pattern of the facts' here—the radii of successive planetary orbits—is undeniably real. The question is: 'Is it significant?' This question is answered by the scientific community, using scientific criteria. The pattern is currently held to be scientifically significant, because it appears to fit into a pattern of efficient *causation*. But Bode's Law might go out of favour again.

What, then, about the *theological* significance of patterns? At a time when astronomy was imbued with a kind of Pythagorean mysticism, a reverence for numbers, Bode's Law might have been interpreted as a reflection of divine harmony in nature: but such theology is now out of fashion. The pattern still exists, but is not held to have theological significance.

Suppose, however (to take a not entirely flippant example) that we wished to point to the theological significance of the extraordinary conjunction of Malcolm Muggeridge's University sermon at St. Giles Cathedral, Edinburgh (14th January, 1968), and the destructive gale that followed it. I need hardly say that the scientific community would find the idea of any causal connection highly implausible; and it is impossible to assign any meaningful 'improbability' to a unique occurrence of this kind. But one *could* use this conjunction to make a theological point (a symbolic sharpening, let us say, of the power and unpredictability of God's judgment), and the theological community *might* accept it. It would then 'extend their knowledge' of God's power and judgment. The pattern is *recognised* by the criteria of that community, and accepted (or rejected) on the basis of reasons and evidence: that is to say, the 'naming' of this event as a 'revelation of God' is an objective matter, related to acknowledged facts. You cannot identify such events by subjective whim: they must maintain an historic continuity. (And note, by the way, that what I have here called a 'revelation of God' could equally have been named 'an act of God': it could be argued that it is the force of the revelation that leads to its being named as an 'act', not the belief in the possibility of an act that leads to its experience as a 'revelation'.)

Now then, to the question: what relationship (if any) are we to expect between these two kinds of pattern in the facts? Considering just the case of temporal sequences of events, there is clearly a range of possibilities:

(a) the two could be entirely independent. Each event in the theological pattern could be a member of some separate causal chain, but no scientifically ascertainable relationship be expected between them. They may, or may not be in a relationship of efficient causation; but this is irrelevant to the theological significance. This is to say more than just that the two 'language games' are autonomous: it is to claim that the cognitive patterns *in reality* are unrelated. Divine patterns cut across causal chains, and the matrix of law and time. We are here dealing with two legitimate ways of 'reading' one complex flux of events. Religious attitudes, thus grounded, are independent of particular scientific findings; 'Revelation of God'—and the naming of 'acts of God'— can proceed in a completely lawful universe. This we may call the 'independence' possibility.

(b) we could take the theological patterns as clues to be followed up —and possibly validated—by scientific analysis. This is to maintain that the only 'real' relationship between events is that sanctioned by science. Theology is a way of keeping us awake, and 'calling on the name of God' a useful reminder of the extent of our ignorance. (The 'coincidence' possibility.)

(c) we could insist that each event in a theological pattern *must* disrupt any causal chain in which science might try to place it. In this view, 'acts of God' are, by definition, interruptions of natural law, ever beyond the scientist's gaze. (The 'interference' possibility.)

(d) we could try to mix these possibilities, and say, for instance, 'sometimes independence, sometimes interference'.

Is the choice between these options *arbitrary*? To say so is to place the matter beyond the reach of reason. But is there any simple 'pattern in the facts' which could decide the issue? Surely not. We are here dealing with much more general shifts of opinion, and the weighing of much less specific factors. Knowledge of the physical structure of the world, by itself, will not remove the necessity of choice. Sometimes theologians have maintained the 'interference' hypothesis; but, at other times (especially in Deist theology), they have found this position abhorrent, and have opted for the 'coincidence' hypothesis. Both these positions have difficulties, as David Hume noticed. As the impersonal analogies and 'general laws' of science began to gain wide currency, and to influence the 'world view', a drift to the 'coincidence' position was understandable; but it failed to maintain a concept of God adequate for religious purposes. At this point, the impulse to name theistic patterns in natural events began to die, and emphasis shifted to inner experience. Judging by the current popularity of 'internalised' and existential theologies, we are now firmly in this reticent phase. But the impulse can return—and with it the necessary theological discipline. This need not be a 'resacralisation', but rather a 'rereading', of the physical world.

Here you will recognise a version of John Wisdom's point about 'gods outside us and within': 'rereading' the physical world will arise in the process of 'coming to know God', as features of the world are used in the discourse. And this leads me to another point, for not only does Barbour not discuss how scientific and theological 'patterns in the facts' might be related in reality, he does not ask whether these patterns may not have a different role within the two languages. Here again, Wisdom's essay is suggestive.

At least one of the objects of identifying a theological 'pattern in the facts' is to attempt to validate or influence an *attitude* to nature; we wish to establish that our hope (or despair) is well-grounded. The pattern is significant to the academic discourse, but it is *also* significant, in a directly personal sense, to the individual who identifies it: to him, furthering the discourse *is* furthering his grasp of a life-orientation. With scientific patterns, this is rarely so: a scientist will find Bode's Law interesting only if it relates to his *scientific* concerns. When a scientific pattern acquires ethical implications, it does so by criteria drawn from outside purely scientific discourse. The scientific community is merely attempting to establish the existence and interrelationship of certain sorts of pattern, although its members are often tempted to use those patterns to justify attitudes. As Stephen Toulmin points out, in his essay on 'Contemporary Scientific Mythology',[5] evolutionary and cosmological theories are particularly

C

prone to acquiring these resonant overtones. Toulmin attacks this tendency vigorously, as a misuse of science; and Barbour remarks, of those who have sought to extract an ethic from Evolution:

> These conclusions seem to depend largely on the prior ethical commitments that lead an author to select particular aspects of evolution as definitive (p. 413).

Is Wisdom (and Barbour) suggesting that theists *should* do this kind of thing? Surely not. Theistic patterns, he points out, relate to our fundamental insecurities. They highlight features of the world which signal, and mediate, both threat and reassurance: and they point to a reconciliation. *Any* simple 'pattern in the facts' (scientific or otherwise) could be incorporated into a theistic system, if its associations relate it to these insecurities. It then becomes a potential source of human bondage, for the sense of threat, or the reassurance, which it brings may be an inappropriate response, from which we must be freed. In directing our attention to their grounding in the facts, Wisdom is *not* advocating that we should now establish, once and for all, an enduring set of patterns, for our everlasting guidance. Quite the reverse. The 'flux of experience' *is* a flux; the patterns come and go. Each new situation is a new situation. We relate it to the past by scanning it for familiar patterns, but to do only this would be a mistake: we must also scan our memory of the past for echoes of the new pattern of the present. Wisdom is pointing more to the possibility of a continual dialogue than to a crucial experiment. By being continually forced to give reasons and indicate evidence, to attempt to grasp a new pattern in each moment, we can be released from inappropriate aspects of our myths and beliefs (by being forced to explore them), and so realise the appropriate aspects. We initiate the 'double and opposite-phased change'.

I hope I have said enough to indicate the reasons for my belief that the roles served by 'patterns of the facts' in theology and science are quite distinct; and also to display my scepticism at establishing any simple relationship between the two. Natural events can acquire a genuine religious significance inasmuch as they develop (symbolise, express, mediate, create) the continuing human struggle for freedom from the tyranny of the gods. ('What do these stones mean to you?') Although perhaps trivial in themselves, cumulatively they provide the genuine reassurance without which we cannot walk the tightrope, maintaining our poise, 'living by faith': or perhaps I should say, since we all carry on living willy-nilly, and seem to have an implicit confidence in just existing, that they help us to *regain* our poise if we

[26]

happen, inadvertently, to glance down. Their total expression constitutes 'religious truth'. Acts of God are named, as legal judgments are delivered, in an attempt to grasp that truth: in neither case is the logical relationship between the statement and the evidence as direct and unequivocal as in scientific discourse. To the religious believer, the many significant patterns of facts in his existence are largely specific to him: they mark out his own salvation, but may be of no direct meaning to a fellow believer. Those significant patterns accepted by the whole religious community are rarer, more obviously spectacular and dramatic, and are described in symbols which are intentionally ambiguous; *from them*, little of specific reference can be *deduced*, but *in them*, a very great deal of individual value can be *related*. They reconcile. In science, what to the individual is significant is also significant to the community, in both detailed patterns and general concepts; and the two are very tightly and unambiguously related.

Now, it is true that *some* scientific evidence *can* legitimately alter *some* statements of religious belief. (The challenge of Darwinism to Biblical literalism is a classic example.) But the extent to which scientific descriptions of events can (and should) invalidate their religious significance can be decided only by an exploration of the criteria by which that significance is assigned in the first place, and of the concepts in which it is expressed. Simple, literal belief in the power of the gods to act as the sole, efficient causes of particular natural events may have been the origin of our God-concept. But many metaphors have been displaced since then, and the power of the Hebrew God to 'render all things down' need no longer rest on such simple minded foundations. The force is now largely imaginative. Is it enough to maintain the religious life? How much (and, precisely, *what*) of the literal 'plain meaning' must remain? Can we meaningfully talk of God's total power to uphold or to destroy without allowing Him the power to act (mysteriously, impenetrably) in 'causing' particular events? And does this talk therefore rely on some limitation on the scientific analysis of causation? These, and many other, fundamental theological issues demand exploration before we can confidently relate our religious and scientific pictures of the natural world.

3. *Implicit metaphysics: metaphor and myth*

Barbour does not discuss these matters. He seems to be insensitive to the more subtle nuances of metaphor: he is much more

[27]

literally-minded. To him, both science and religion refer to something *structural* and permanent in the world, and it is 'one world', in which events are events, and causes, causes. He is suitably cautious:

> Religious beliefs refer to all events—but only insofar as they are related to ultimate concern (p. 261).

or again:

> Religious beliefs should be evaluated primarily as interpretations of historical events, religious experience, and life-situations; any contribution they make to a broader synthesis or metaphysical system should be viewed more cautiously (p. 262).

But, although he sets out (in part 3 of his book) to analyse particular problems, using an approach based on the premise that science and religion are independent 'alternative languages', he adds:

> But in each case we will not stop with such a solution; we will go on to ask about the structures of man and the world which make such diverse languages appropriate. We will attempt to formulate a coherent interpretation of experience (p. 269).

In other words, Barbour has committed himself to a search for a set of metaphysical categories to relate the 'patterns in the facts', the 'structures of man and the world'. What he sees as necessary is some basic model in which scientific and religious talk can be seen as literal descriptions of aspects of one process: the scientist says 'it was caused by atomic collisions', and the religious man says 'it was caused by God', and, when we look at the event in detail, we find— why, yes, atomic collisions *were* involved, but also some other influence which doesn't yield to that analysis. Perhaps the motive for the search for such a model never arises rationally from the evidence: it is judged by results.

But before we look at Barbour's suggested synthesis, I want to make some remarks about metaphysics in general.

Kepler is alleged to have made a statement which sums up the scientific metaphysical takeover bid: 'The universe is not similar to a divine living organism, but rather is similar to a clock'.

What most people notice in that sentence is that Kepler proposes a new 'root metaphor' for a metaphysics: for organism, read clock. But perhaps what we should notice is the care with which Kepler twice uses the phrase 'similar to': he did *not* say (as later men did) the universe *is* not a divine living organism, but *is* a clock.

Douglas Berggren, in a recent and important essay on 'The Use and Abuse of Metaphor',[6] discusses the role of such metaphors in metaphysics. His main points are worth repeating here:

(a) A metaphor must, by definition, be held to be *literally absurd*. A poet need not propound that 'man is a wolf', if this is already a commonplace literal belief: he would not be saying anything.

(b) A metaphor is viable because of some perceived or felt similarity between the two equated objects; but if these similarities could be exhaustively catalogued and stated, the metaphor would be 'dead'. It is used because it sets a puzzle, and suggests to its hearer all kinds of *possible* relations: here, in another form, are Wisdom's 'unspoken connections'. On hearing that 'man is a wolf', we do not say 'You mean that man is like a wolf in respects A, B, C . . ., but unlike a wolf in respects X, Y, Z . . .: yes, I agree'.

(c) Related to (b) is Berggren's key idea that metaphor involves a kind of 'stereoscopic vision'. The two images are, as it were, simultaneously laid on reality with an irreducible *tension*. We do not view man from our normal stance, then switch to seeing him as a wolf, note a few similarities, and then switch back to our original viewpoint, carrying what we have learned with us. The one organism is seen in both perspectives at *once*: the pro-pounding of the metaphor not only *reflects* similarities, it can also *create* them.[3] After the stereoscopic vision, we see men as more wolfish, and wolves as more human.

(d) Myth arises when a metaphor, a literal absurdity, is held to be *literally true*, the absurdity remaining unrecognised; as when, for instance, we hold that 'Christ was God' (or that 'Poverty is Violence').

In both scientific models and metaphysical systems, single metaphors are extended to encompass all relevant phenomena (in metaphysics, *all* phenomena). The realist holds that this is a descriptive exercise: in doing this rigorously, we get a firmer grasp on what things are *really like*. However, since the late nineteenth century, the naïve realist in science has had a severe shock: when it became clear that the universe *wasn't* a clock (or a billiard table), many philosophers of science renounced any realist claims at all. Barbour opts for what he calls 'critical realism'—which is, roughly, to say that we are, in science, gradually improving our descriptions of the way things are, but, of course, we realise that it's not *quite* as simple as that. . . .

And yet knowing you mustn't be naïve isn't good enough: I suggest that knowing that you must hold all vital metaphors in tension is. However plausible one root metaphor may be, and however cautiously you embrace it, that single embrace is the irredeemable sin. The trouble with metaphysicians is that they are traditionally monogamous.

> Berggren, towards the end of his essay, suggests this conclusion: While it is possible to develop a literal or univocal language for spatial reality, and while an equally univocal language for non-spatial reality is also at least theoretically conceivable, their philosophically necessary interconnections or correlations can be formulated only in terms of vital metaphors. . . . While construing one mode of reality in terms of the other, the autonomy of each must be preserved even while they are being simultaneously assimilated or integrated. . . . In a sense, therefore, it is not the machine, diagram, portrait, or specimen, but stereoscopic vision itself which must become the most fundamental root metaphor of metaphysics.

This is what we might call 'Ximenes-metaphysics'. The metaphor of stereoscopic vision defines the nature of the puzzle. My own view is that it is the function of the symbolism continued in religious language to support and maintain the *tension* inherent in solving the puzzle, for it is a fact of history that the tension is exceedingly difficult to maintain, and man lapses naturally into myth—into, in Blake's words, 'Single vision, and Newton's sleep'. This, I take it, is the inner logic of radical monotheism.

However, before returning finally to Barbour, I want to make three comments on Berggren's ideas:

(*a*) The atheistic scientific materialist attempts a total redescription of nature in terms of simple physical metaphors: clocks, billiard tables, waves on ponds, law-abiding populations. He is very often a naïve realist: the categories demanded by this metaphysics are, to him, *all that there is*. In trying to refute him, many people try to argue that he is simply wrong, in that things happen which cannot be accounted for in his analysis. I suggest this tactic is mistaken. The materialist is right: his metapho fits; but he is also wrong, in that other metaphors can also fit, and draw attention to other features. In other words, 'there is more to be said'.

Perhaps an analogy might help here. Suppose a group are discussing what constitutes a 'game'. They have the usual problem over the definition, so they settle on one paradigm case that they all agree to accept as a 'game'. They opt for Association Football. But then one of them says: 'But soccer isn't a game—it's big business'. The question is: does this refute what they had previously agreed? Surely not: all the features that make soccer a game remain, and are accepted. What our obtuse objector has done is to emphasise further features of the scene—admittedly, features that are largely operative *behind* the scenes, but which are still reflected on the playing field. (Who has not heard of 'needle' in a match, when the result is crucial to 'getting into Europe'?) The 'truth', of course, is that Soccer is neither a game, nor big business, but 22 men and a referee running round a rectangular patch of grass, kicking and heading a leather ball. But who would bother to watch *that*? (One is reminded of Wisdom's remark that metaphysicians are either paradoxical or boring—with the majority, unfortunately, in the latter category.)

(*b*) Professor R. W. Hepburn, in a broadcast talk[7] let slip this speculation:

> May not (an) ambivalence run throughout the whole field of our experience and its interpretation; so that in the end we have a choice between two equally possible readings of an ambiguous total pattern—a sceptical reading or a theistic reading? It may be so; but in order to be sure, one would need to attain something which I am very far indeed from attaining, a bird's-eye view of both options with all their ramifications.

There, unless I am gravely mistaken, speaks the man of single vision. If a theistic pattern is remotely viable as a metaphor for one eye, then stereoscopic vision will suffuse it throughout our whole perception. Our two eyes make theists of us all. Once the metaphor has had a life, and genuinely guided people's perception, what it referred to can never be lost. The whole world is, at least in some measure, Goddish. And only by keeping both eyes open (and, one might add, freeing one's hands) will we ever be able to assess the damage.

(c) To take a natural event, and to overlay it with a theistic pattern, so that we say 'It is an act of God', is, surely, to make a metaphorical assertion. Whatever it conveys of genuine value, it is a literal absurdity. And we cannot expect to make sense of the claim in literal terms, or in a mythic metaphysics.

Professor Hepburn, again, puts the point clearly:

What exactly is the problem—the problem of anchoring and grounding the gospel? With (many) theologians . . . concrete historicity does matter: Jesus' rising from the dead, for instance, is to be accepted as hard, historical fact. Is not that enough as an anchor for the structure of images? I fear it is not enough. For the rising of Jesus to become gospel, it has to be taken as *God's act of raising him from the dead* and not the bare story of a man's resuscitation. And before we can meaningfully interpret it in this distinctive way—as God acting—we must know what we are saying with the words 'God acting'. An appeal to the hardest facts of history cannot help us here.

4. *Acts of God*

We come now to Barbour's suggested synthesis. In the light of what I have already said, my objections to it should be fairly clear, so I will merely outline it, and make two specific comments.

From a mass of modern scientific data, Barbour sees the emergence of a 'new view of nature', which, he says, 'forces us to re-examine our ideas of God's relation to the world'. He is impressed by the 'dynamic and temporal character of a growing, evolving universe'; by the realisation, at all levels of scientific analysis, that 'the whole is greater than the sum of the parts', and that events often appear to be less than fully determined by antecedent causes. As a critical realist, he takes these scientific results as representing the character of things, rather than just our ignorance or blindness. He advocates a 'metaphysics of levels', with man as a 'many-levelled unity', and the biblical idea of the essentially social character of selfhood reinstated: 'a person is constituted by his relationships . . .'. He suggests the merging of the traditional doctrines of creation and providence into a doctrine of 'continuing creation': the universe is still 'coming into being'. But, above all, he opts, as his metaphysical scheme, for Whitehead's 'process philosophy', which allows for novelty and freedom, as well as lawfulness, at all levels of reality. Basically, this metaphysics takes as its 'root-metaphor' the concept of the organism, as seen in an open-ended evolutionary perspective (unlike

[32]

the medieval metaphysics, which was rooted in a kind of static, essentially complete, organism). Its basic unit is 'the event'. Every new occurrence is seen as a present response (self-cause) to past events (efficient cause), in terms of potentialities grasped (final cause). With these categories, the whole of nature can be represented as a dynamic organic process.

Barbour opens his final chapter with what he takes to be the key questions:

> How can God act if the world is governed by scientific laws? What is God's relation to the causal processes of nature? ... Can we still accept the idea of providence, God's governance of nature and history? How is divine sovereignty operative in the midst of the natural forces by which we explain events today? Is a prayer for rain appropriate—does God influence meteorological processes? Again, is the concept of immanence, God as present and active in the world, compatible with the scientific understanding of nature?

As Barbour points out, the dominant modern viewpoint combines a deistic, 'non-interventionist', representation of the God/Nature relation, with an existentialist understanding of God's action in the sphere of personal selfhood. But Barbour insists on a more precise description of *how* God can be said to 'act':

> As an example of the dilemma, consider the deliverance of Israel at the Red Sea. According to the commonest interpretation today, this was not a supernatural miracle, but a 'strong East wind' ... which might easily have been explained as a natural phenomenon, but which Israel 'interpreted as God's action'. Does God then, act in *all* winds, though only certain people are aware of it? Or does He act in *no* winds, but only in the religious response of a people? Or does he act in *some* winds *and* in the interpretation thereof? If 'event as interpreted' is said to be the locus of revelation, how do we avoid emphasising the interpretive activity more than the event in the world, so that the object of our study is Israel's faith rather than God's acts? Is divine sovereignty then reduced to 'the inward incitement of a religious response to an ordinary event'? (p. 420).

Barbour classifies three groups of theological answers. The first consist of those who maintain the classical view of God as 'Sovereign Ruler of the Created Order'. This includes Barth and the neo-Thomists, and they are criticised, not surprisingly, also on classical grounds—problems of evil and human freedom. Barth is also criticised for failing to find metaphysical categories to portray God's action in nature—categories 'that can be related to the terms in which the scientist describes the world'.

The second group consists of existentialist and linguistic views, which all deny God's activity in nature: this includes Bultmann and Heim. Barbour's criticism of this group is already clear.

The third group consists of 'Process Views': Whitehead and Hartshorne. Both see God as 'an influence on the world process', but the extent of that influence is drastically reduced from the classical view. To Whitehead, God is 'Creative Persuasion'; to Hartshorne, 'Sympathetic Participant'. Barbour sees these ideas as a potential solution to his problem.

I confine myself to two brief comments:

(a) it is not clear to me that these views solve Barbour's dilemma of (for instance) the Red Sea miracle. As Barbour admits, since God, in Whitehead's view, is just one influence among many, God's acts in the world 'are not readily detectable'. And this is reinforced by Daniel Williams' comment: 'To assign any particular historical event to God's specific action in the world is to risk ultimate judgment on our assertions. Faith leads us to take the risk' (quoted on p. 448). In other words, events still have to be interpreted and *named*. It helps us not at all that we have cleverly devised a little scheme into which a 'supernatural' influence might be poured: since we cannot penetrate the event, the matter remains as mysterious as before. Indeed, I do not see how *any* description of how God acts can help us. By the time we have *recognised* the event, it is too late to investigate how it came about. And knowing how it might have come about does not, in any way, help us to name it. Hepburn's difficulty remains.

(b) the restriction on God's sovereignty is such that I doubt whether the word 'God' is appropriate. To inspire worship, God must be held to be powerful; is Whitehead's God any more useful than Aristotle's God or the Deist God as a viable religious object? It is hard to avoid the impression that process philosophy is resacralising the world with a nice, kind, liberal American.

As Barbour very rightly says:

Perhaps in addition to the 'persuasive' aspects of God there are more active and authoritarian aspects, to which the sense of inescapable judgment and overwhelming awe in religious experience testify (p. 448).

[34]

I take this criticism to be decisive. We cannot throw away the most vital religious insight of radical monotheism. Theology must relate to the experience of those who search for their freedom: and we *fear* our freedom. The fear must be expressed and incorporated in the tradition, if it is to be transcended. I do not recognise process philosophy as a system of *religious* thought, for it pays no attention to the extremities of our experience. If our metaphysical imagination can do no better than this, then we should pay little attention to it.

My conclusion is that Barbour's attempt at a 'coherent interpretation of experience' is premature. The issue he raises is clearly the central theological issue raised by modern science: but I do not believe that he has grasped its true nature.

When the literally-held myths which have grounded a system of religious thought come to be seen for the absurdities that they are, the proper response is not to abandon them, but to retain them as imaginative, metaphorical constructs. Indeed, it is *only* when they are seen thus that the cognitive insights they may contain are available to us. You might say, paradoxically, that religious 'beliefs' are only useful to us when they are no longer 'believed in'. The natural reaction to this situation is to look for a new myth, a grounding which is literally firm. Judging by much modern theology, it looks as if atheism is that myth. But perhaps the call of God is that we should remain in the desert: that there is *no* literal 'promised land'; that tension, metaphor and stereoscopic vision is our inescapable lot; that we can only 'live by faith'.

The question of the putative 'Death of God' is then *not* whether God's existence can be made literally plausible, but whether the many symbolic presentations of God's presence have all (and simultaneously) been reduced to *dead metaphor*. And *that* is quite a different matter.

References:

1. Ian G. Barbour, *Issues in Science and Religion* (S.C.M. Press, 1966 and 1968).
2. John Wisdom, 'Gods', in *Philosophy and Psychoanalysis* (Blackwell, 1953).
3. Several similar examples are discussed in Donald Schon, *Displacement of Concepts* (Tavistock, 1963).
4. Paul van Buren, 'On Doing Theology', in G. N. A. Vesey (ed.), *Talk of God* (Macmillan, 1969).
5. in Alastair McIntyre (ed.), *Metaphysical Beliefs* (S.C.M. Press, 1957). See also Erwin N. Hilbert, 'The Uses and Abuses of Thermodynamics in Religion', *Daedalus*, 95, 4, Fall 1966, pp. 1046–1080; and A. G. N. Flew, *Evolutionary Ethics* (Macmillan, 1968).
6. Douglas Berggren, 'The Use and Abuse of Metaphor I and II', *Review of Metaphysics*, Vol. 16, 1962–3, pp. 237–258, 450–472.
7. in 'Religion and Humanism' (B.B.C., 1964).

Science, Society and the Churches

R. A. Buchanan

What I have to say in this paper falls into two distinct parts. The first part is concerned with some reflections on the nature of religion, both because this is the first of a series of lectures on the general theme of science and religion, so that some preliminary discussion about definitions is appropriate, and because I have recently been revising my own ideas about religion and irreligion. The second part will be concerned more particularly with the historical impact of science on organised Christian religion. I hope in this way to open up some of the general and particular aspects of our theme and to set it in an overall historical perspective.

Whether one speaks of the 'Death of God' or continues to speak of God in the traditional terms and images, most contemporary discussion about religion tends to take for granted the conventional framework of such discourse. My object here is to call this framework into question, and to argue that a proper understanding of the role of religion in modern society requires a readiness to go back to first principles about both religion and the nature of our society. I am convinced that the conventional religious assumptions about Life and Death, Heaven and Hell, God and Man, are no longer valid in a civilisation which has been transformed by ideological and social revolutions. It is not God who has died but religion itself, in the sense in which this term has customarily been interpreted. The organisations of conventional religion may live on for a generation or more by a process of institutional inertia, but to all effective purposes they have become irrelevant. If there is any hope of a resurrection of religion, it is only on

[36]

condition that the concept of religion undergoes a radical re-assessment.

Religion has always been a complex phenomenon, subsuming a range of cultural, political, sociological, and moral functions in addition to the ritual activities calculated to relieve fear by the propitiation of real or imaginary forces. In primitive societies these functions merged together so that, for example, the witch-doctor of a Red Indian tribe usually had significant politico-social powers as well as being indispensable in his medical and priestly capacities. The differentiation of these functions became clear with the increasing specialisation practised in early civilizations, but for long the priest remained a figure of outstanding power in the determination of policy and in the definition of morality. In the civilisation of ancient Egypt the pharaohs were priest-kings, surrounding themselves in the aura of divinity, and in Sumeria the priest-caste used its monopoly of the new mysteries of civilised communities—the skills of literacy and numeracy—to influence political life. In the Old Testament—a superb document of the social and political evolution of a nation—the dominant role of the priests is clearly demonstrated, at least until the Kingdom of David.

With the gradual extension of man's control over his environment and the consequent recession of the realm of magic, the role of religious institutions such as priests, temples, and churches has become increasingly specific, while the other specialised aspects of social activity have become secularised. This, however, has been a very slow process, so that religious institutions have rarely been faced with the necessity of abandoning their claims to influence political and social decisions. Even today, rites of coronation and investiture preserve fragments of priestly power in British government, while church schools, church marriage services, and clerical pronouncements on questions of morality perpetuate other roles of religion even though they have become extremely attenuated. However threadbare such functions have become, it is useful to distinguish them in order to clear the ground for a definition of religion. In the first place, religion has traditionally performed a cultural function in the preservation and transmission of civilisation. The priest-clerks of early civilisations recorded the knowledge of their societies on stones and tablets of clay, passing it on to their descendants. In the Dark Ages of Medieval Europe, the Christian monasteries preserved the memories of classical

[37]

civilisation in their libraries and transmitted it to the new civilisation of Western Europe. And throughout the history of Western Civilisation, the churches have played an important part in the development of educational institutions and in the attainment of cultural continuity.

Secondly, religion has usually been an important socio-political force, contributing to social stability and cohesion. Whether one regards this as a valuable 'social cement' maintaining proper public order, or as a deplorable 'opiate of the people' is largely a matter of political taste—the contribution itself is undeniable. From ancient societies until modern times the attribution of divine approval to the powers that be has made religion a valuable asset of government. Extreme forms of this cohesive sanction can be found in the influence of the Mosaic Law in the formation of the first Hebrew state to the support of the Catholic Church for the government of General Franco in modern Spain, but it has been generally true that religion has exercised a politically stabilising influence in all societies, even though it must be admitted that Christianity has been more prolific than most major religions in inspiring sectarian, chiliastic, movements which have been powerful revolutionary forces at particular times and places. The study of such sects has shown that they rarely retain their revolutionary fervour for more than a single generation, so that although they have not been historically insignificant they must be regarded as exceptions from the normal pattern of religious political action.

Thirdly, religion has been a factor of profound moral significance in all human societies. Religious leaders have generally claimed the prerogative of defining moral and ethical norms. This is not just a matter of determining legal codes, although this has been important. Religion has also fixed moral values and social customs, deciding issues of right and wrong, or good and bad behaviour. Thus the Christian Church in Medieval Europe established acceptable standards for the pursuit of war, industry, and commerce. The fact that it was occasionally over-ruled by secular forces, as in the instance of the rules against usury, did not destroy the moral claims of religion, even though such occasions represented important points at which the authority of Medieval Christendom was eroded.

There have, of course, been other functions of religion, although most of them are capable of being included in one or other of those already discussed. The most important of the functions which will not fit into one of the former categories is that of providing personal consolation, through prayer and sacrament, religious service and ritual, for the individual who accepts the authority of religious organisations and their ability to give him such consolation. Whether or not this is a rational process is, for the moment, beside the point, which is that one of the great strengths of traditional religion has been its success in persuading many people that it possesses the gift of salvation. To those who accept its authority, a religious organisation is able to offer the promise of eternal life or the threat of eternal damnation—and the negative sanction has frequently been even more important than the positive one.

To distinguish the traditional functions of religion is not necessarily to define it, and as the scope of religion has been so wide any definition must be somewhat arbitrary. Before deciding on such an arbitrary definition, therefore, it will be useful to consider the role of the traditional religious functions in contemporary society. The one fact which dominates any such consideration is that all the functions which have been discussed so far have declined significantly in importance in modern industrial societies. They have degenerated into mere vestiges of their former importance under the corrosive actions of modern ideas and a rising standard of living. The cultural and politico-social functions have become almost completely secularised, which is to say that religion has ceased to exercise any meaningful part in them. Religious organisations still claim to assert a moral authority, but the claim is largely unheeded and in default of any alternative authority modern society appears to be moving into a condition of moral relativism. The personal function of religion in offering spiritual consolation to individuals is still important, but only for the diminishing band of followers who accept the validity of the offer.

In all its major aspects, therefore, religion finds itself, in Western Civilisation in the second half of the twentieth century, on the defensive. Not only are its traditional functions being undermined: it also finds that the powerful solvent of modern ideas is eroding the images and dogmas in which Christianity has been expressed for the greater part of two millenia. Doctrines which have been believed for generations are now no longer believed. Indeed, they have become unbelievable because modern man is no longer able to accept the magical assumptions and suspensions of reason which are essential to them. This is not to argue that modern man is a paragon of virtue and rationality. Clearly he is

[39]

no *better* in an absolute moral sense than those who have gone before him, and he is capable of lapsing into weird fantasies and superstitions like his predecessors. But modern man is *different*. His ideas have been framed in an environment which is qualitatively different from that of his predecessors, and part of the intellectual fabric of that environment is the supremacy of reason and the rejection of magic. So religion expressed in terms which are irrational and magical has become absurd to modern man, and a faith which is equated with credulity is no longer acceptable to him. When the author of the Fourth Gospel inserted the story of Thomas's refusal to believe until he could see and touch his Risen Lord, he might have been anticipating this habit of mind of modern man. The Thomas syndrome is now paramount. Modern man must be convinced by arguments which are consonant with his reason. Otherwise he will reject claims to religious authority, or at least suspend judgment on them.

We have had to make generalisations about the species 'modern man' in order to show the main lines of our argument. It will be necessary to fill out and justify these generalisations in our discussion. Meanwhile, we must return to the task of defining religion. If the account given so far can be accepted as a reasonably accurate factual statement despite the high degree of generalisation, it may at least be agreed that the traditional functions of religion have declined in importance. It has to be asked, therefore, in what if anything of the remaining ruins of these functions does twentieth century religion consist? If the answer is made in terms of giving personal consolation to the remnant of believers, then religion will have only a vestigial and quietist role in modern society and may be ignored as a determinative factor in the great world issues of the present generation. If, however, the answer is made in terms of recreating a role of cultural, politico-social, or moral significance for the organisations of traditional religion, it is an unrealistic answer because the institutions of modern society are unlikely to renounce readily the autonomy which they have gained, often after many centuries of struggle against religious authoritarianism. Any religion which attempts to turn back the tide of secularisation is attempting the impossible. Secularisation, indeed, is not necessarily irreligious, any more than science, technology, or the use of reason, and it is a profound mistake of conventional religion to regard it as such. The standard responses of traditional religious organisations to the problem of re-defining the role of religion in terms appropriate to the later decades of the twentieth century are thus inadequate and spring from an understanding of religion itself which is too narrow. In order to look with any real hope to future role for religion, it is necessary first to re-assess the content of religion.

Fundamentally, religion is concerned with something beyond its traditional functions and conventional dogmas. It is concerned with the aims, the goals, the purpose of human life, and with the behaviour related to a conscious pursuit of these aims. However much the 'superstructure' of religion may change, the need for such 'basic religion' will remain of paramount importance for the orientation of individuals and of society. The implications of such a definition of religion are important. It means, in the first place, that anybody with a clear sense of purpose in life, whether it be the pursuit of money, beauty, or the service of one's fellow men, is included within the terms of having a religion, from which it follows that the types of religion are enormously extended. Secondly, this definition of 'basic religion' means that the concept of religion is stripped of its supernatural and magical associations, unless these are consciously incorporated into the aims or 'belief system' of the individual. This is to say that there is no need for a person who accepts a religion in this sense to put his rational faculties into suspended animation: belief in the power of reason may, indeed, become a potent and important religion, as it does in the case of many scientists. Thirdly, this definition of religion means that the conventional distinction between religion and irreligion becomes more usually a distinction between religions, while irreligion becomes something other than an attack upon conventional religion. The militant atheist or humanist who lashes organised religion is, in the terms of this definition, as religious as the people he attacks. Irreligion becomes instead a condition, familiar enough in the modern world, of aimlessness or constantly changing short-term aims. For the genuinely irreligious person, life is deprived of depth and significance because he can find no stable purpose in it. Irreligion is thus a pathological condition from which the only escape other than death is the discovery of some meaning or purpose by which life may be orientated.

It may be objected that a definition of religion which deprived the concept of any supernatural connotation is a denial of the accepted meaning of the term. There are two lines along which this objection may be answered. The first is to review once more

D

the wide variety of functions to which the word 'religion' has referred in the past, and to argue the advantages of having a definition which can be easily understood while going to the heart of most religious activities by stressing the importance of a sense of purpose. The second line along which the objection to the extension of the notion of religion may be answered, is to accept the complaint that this is an unusual definition of religion, but to point out that we live in an unusual society in which old norms of behaviour have disappeared and in which the traditional functions of religion have little place. To insist on a supernatural element in religion is to consign the term to the history books, so that it will become a concept like 'feudalism', which once had great vitality but has no relevance to social life in Western Civilisation today. Conventional religion is dead. Individuals may go on feeling a sense of awe and wonder at the confrontation of the numinous in nature or in worship (there is an important psychological aspect to the personal function of traditional religion), but it is inconceivable—for better or for worse—that such conventional religious experience will ever again play a significant part in the determination of modern society. Any hope for a resurrection of religion in contemporary society resides in the possibility of expressing it in a way which is acceptable to a scientific and secular age. In maintaining that religion is about *purpose in life* we are exploring the extent of this possibility.

Just as I have attempted to define 'religion', it is as well to give a working definition of 'science' to understand the way I am using the term. Science as we know it today is a product of the scientific revolution of the sixteenth and seventeenth centuries, when there occurred for the first time a fusion of various elements which, although they had existed partially and independently before, had never previously been brought into close relationship. For the sake of brevity and at the risk of gross over-simplification, these elements may be regarded as three in number. In the first place, there is the fundamental scientific exercise of collecting information carefully and classifying it. This exercise depends upon faculties of literacy and numeracy and thus only occurs where some degree of 'civilisation' has been achieved. The Sumerian and Egyptian astronomers were probably the first people to undertake such a task systematically and successfully, and deserve considering as the first scientists on that account. But they were not scientists in the modern sense because their skills as observers and classifiers were as yet unrelated to the other two elements which we have to consider. The second element is the faculty of deductive reasoning, by which I mean the ability to think in a sophisticated manner, using abstract symbols and concepts, in order to construct rational systems or models on the basis of axioms which are taken as assumed. The powers of the logician and the geometrician are of this deductive type: the latter for instance, is capable of constructing an abstruse system on the ground of a few simple assumptions such as 'Let the shortest distance between two points be a straight line'. The Greek scientists developed and exercised these deductive powers to high degree, but as with their Sumerian predecessors this did not make them 'modern' scientists. The third element is that of inductive reasoning. This is the quality of experimental analysis, of subjecting observations to progressive examination in order to modify and add to them. It is frequently called the empirical method, and like the other elements in science it was present in antiquity in the work of Archimedes and even in some aspects of the wide-ranging genius of Aristotle. Unlike the other elements, however, the empirical method only attained full expression in the scientific revolution. To flourish properly it requires a sound basis of classified observations and a good training in the rational skills. Logically, as well as historically, therefore, it was the final element to reach maturity and modern science has thus sometimes been characterised as the application of inductive reasoning alone. The great experimental work of Galileo and Francis Bacon gives some substance to this claim. But the scientific revolution was also distinguished by the mathematical-rational inspiration of men such as Descartes and Newton, and by a host of lesser figures (e.g. Robert Boyle, John Ray), who devoted themselves largely to the fundamental scientific exercise of making careful observations. Modern science, therefore, should be seen as a fusion or amalgam of these diverse elements, occurring for the first time in the history of mankind when it occurred in Western Europe in the sixteenth-seventeenth centuries.

This is not the place to give an account of the scientific revolution, important and fascinating though this development has been. Suffice it to say for our purposes that from very small beginnings in the sixteenth century the new intellectual habits of mind which derived from modern science have spread throughout Europe and the world, affecting an ever increasing proportion of the population and raising considerable problems of adjustment for the older, pre-scientific traditions of thought. Amongst these, and paramount in a consideration of the intellectual shift in modern Europe, are the institutions of the Christian religion. There is, of course, no *necessary* conflict between the interpretation of religion —at least in the sense in which I have defined it—and that of modern science. But in historical fact the Christian churches have frequently found themselves defending undefensible positions in the dialogue with modern science which began with the Copernican theory of the heliocentric universe in the sixteenth century and which has been continuing ever since. It would be too large a task for the present compass to attempt to trace the successive stages in this uneven dialogue over four centuries. For my purposes in this brief review it will be convenient to look at the impact of modern science on the institutions and traditions of Christianity under four headings. Once again, there is a serious danger of over-simplification, but at least it should provide some headings for our subsequent discussion.

The first heading is the new sense of space introduced into the intellectual system of Western Civilisation by the scientific revolution. Even if the homely notion of a 'three tier' universe, with the flat earth balanced between heaven above and hell below, had become nothing more than a part of the intimate folk lore of the time, the best intellects of the pre-Copernican period still accepted the Ptolemaic model of the earth-centred universe, sustained by Aristotelian dynamics. The model was closed, small-scale, and— so far as the earth was concerned—static. The Copernican model, on the other hand, opened out the system indefinitely and intro- duced an un-nerving dynamic quality which was repugnant to tradition and was consequently vigorously opposed, with the churches, it need hardly be added, joining vociferously in the opposition. But then came Galileo Galilei, wielding the telescope as a new tool of scientific discovery, claiming to have demonstrated by his observations the validity of the Copernican hypothesis. Still the traditionalists withstood the scandalous innovation, but the weight of scientific observation was too strong for them and within a generation the new and vastly increased scale of the universe had been accepted and Newton had clinched the mathe- matical explanation of how the new model operated. In our own century, the scale of the universe has increased to infinity, and the stature of man has been correspondingly decreased. The churches, like everybody else, have been compelled to come to terms with this scientific revelation, even if they have frequently done so with a bad grace.

The second impact of science on religion has been in imparting a new sense of time. It is not only space which has become infinite: time also seems to have lost its beginning and its end. It was not always so. Until little more than a century ago, the traditional view was that the universe was some five or six thousand years old, and that it would come to an end with the completion of the seventh millenium, even though there was some uncertainty as to when this would be. Most people, intellectuals as well as the proverbial men in the street, accepted the calculations of Archbishop Usher, to the effect that the world was created in 4004 B.C., without question. Even Newton, whose genius had rendered the new scientific space scale explicable and acceptable, followed the traditional time scale without demur. It was not until the beginning of the nineteenth century that the scientific study of geology began to raise doubts, because a tremendous increase in the time scale became necessary in order to make sense of the systematic observation of rock strata, fossils, and the processes of natural erosion. The parallel development of biology had the same effect, requiring much more time than was available in the traditional 7,000 year span to explain the evolution and selection of species. Once again the traditionalists resisted, and once again the churches stood with the traditionalists. Bishop Wilberforce went to the barricades in defence of the traditional assumptions. And once again, within a generation, the weight of scientific evidence had made opposition intellectually impossible, so that we have had to accustom ourselves to a new and near-infinite time scale of many billions of years. Science, of course, has not solved the mystery of time, the concept of which remains elusive and ambiguous. It has simply made us think in terms of much more time than anybody had imagined possible before the scientific revolution.

In altering our spatial and temporal categories, modern science has struck at some of the fundamental bastions of traditionalist thought—which means particularly at the thought of our religious institutions. But the third area of impact is, if anything, even more profound. The scientific revolution has turned our ideas of authority upside down, and has condemned traditionalism as being intellectually unrespectable. The traditional view is the authoritarian view, which is to say what is, is right. It is the deferential attitude—the reference back to the book, to the Bible, to the

Church, to the past Master, to Aristotle, to Galen, and so on —which characterises the authoritarian, traditional habit of mind. Modern science, on the other hand, starts at the opposite end of the argument, accepting no statement or observation unless it has been tested, and then only on a provisional basis pending further analysis. This approach is profoundly antipathetic towards traditionalism, towards magic, or towards any form of super-or-supranaturalism. The conflict was apparent in Galileo's famous dispute with the Vatican astronomers, when the latter refused to look through Galileo's telescope because they could not bring themselves to believe that this piece of glass and leather could refute the authority of Ptolemy, unchallenged for over a thousand years and hallowed by centuries of endorsement by Church Fathers and other intellectual eminences. It just could not be. It went against the grain of common assumptions. Yet it had to be, and the common assumptions had to change, albeit slowly for we are all traditionalists at heart and we all have to undergo our personal scientific revolution. This, I suppose, is why the publication of *Honest to God* caused such a furore, and it is why the Roman Catholic Church is now quaking with unprecedented convulsions. Modern science is driving us to think for ourselves and to make our judgments untramelled by traditionalist notions of authority.

There is a fourth area of impact of science on religion which should be taken into account, although it is too large a field to do anything except mention briefly. This is the fact that science has contributed in large measure to the emergence of a new type of society. It is a society which is dynamic rather than static, forward looking rather than backward looking, rich rather than poor. It is scarcely being fanciful to claim that modern science and technology have made possible the increased productivity of wealth and thereby the emergence in Western Civilisation of those conditions of comparative affluence which bring within the attainment of ordinary men and women the 'good life' that has previously only been available to the privileged minority. It cannot be denied that this new science-inspired society has found itself confronted by a whole range of new problems and a more sophisticated version of old ones such as crime. But it cannot be denied either that many of the traditional problems have disappeared or are disappearing. Poverty, for example, is a much diminished problem today (though none the less a social disgrace where it remains), and with its decline he old 'ambulance' functions of the churches have atrophied.

[46]

Many churches, indeed have found the adjustment to the new society extraordinarily difficult, which accounts in part for the large number of derelict church buildings, converted to warehouses or bingo halls, in the great cities of this country. To survive in the affluent society the churches need to acquire a new critique, giving them a fresh social purpose.

It is not my commission, however, to make out a blue-print for the survival of the churches, even if I think that such a blue-print is attainable. But I hope that I have said enough to show the sort of issues which confront religion today, both in the general sense of re-defining the nature and purpose of religion, and in the particular sense of adjusting to the profound intellectual and material changes which the scientific revolution has wrought in our society. If I have said enough to stimulate a discussion of these fundamental issues, I will be satisfied.

Science and Christian Apologetics

Anthony Barnard

In the preface to a collection of essays, T. H. Huxley, a leading proponent of Darwinism in the latter half of the last century, wrote the following:

> I had set out on a journey, with no other purpose than that of exploring a certain province of natural knowledge; I strayed no hair's breadth from the course which it was my right and my duty to pursue; and yet I found that, whatever route I took, before long, I came to a tall and formidable-looking fence. Confident as I might be in the existence of an ancient and indefeasible right of way, before me stood the thorny barrier with its comminatory notice-board—'No Thoroughfare, By Order. Moses'. There seemed no way over; nor did the prospect of creeping round, as I saw some do, attract me. The only alternatives were to give up my journey—which I was not minded to do—or to break down the fence and go through it.[1]

It is difficult to be certain how obvious the conflict, which Huxley saw between science and religion, is in the minds of people today, but I suspect that in much popular understanding the two are seen to be mutually exclusive, and that though Christians either fail to see the problem or imagine that they have reached a satisfactory understanding of the inter-relationship of the two, the church is woefully ill-equipped to speak the faith in a scientific and technological age. My aim will be to examine the problem, which Huxley so elegantly described, and, I hope, to reach somewhat different conclusions from his own. The problem is raised, in the first instant, by the fact that the scientist and the Christian both speak about life, but do so in entirely different languages. The Christian speaks in abstract terms, about faith and God, about miracle and spirit, about revelation and commitment. The scientist speaks in concrete terms about fact and law, about experiment and observation. Yet, problematic though it may be to relate these two approaches, the difference, of course goes much deeper than this. The Christian doctrine of man sees him as created by God, in His image, to be in a special relationship to himself, which sets him apart from the rest of creation, over which he has dominion. Man is described as rejecting this dependent and yet responsible role, and so as rejecting God and being in a fallen state. From this state God in his love calls him, offering him reconciliation through the blood of Christ, acceptance, fulfilment and life eternal. Significantly, this summary statement of Christian belief, is integrally related to the words of the Bible, and more particularly to the opening chapters of Genesis, which were believed to come from the hand of Moses. Here, in these chapters, we read the story of creation, fall and flood, and learn of the origin of language and race. Clearly then, the advance of knowledge about the origin and procession of life was easily circumscribed by Biblical revelation, by the words of Moses, and it is reasonable to suppose, as Huxley goes on to say, that:

> The credentials of one who exercises control over the operations of the reasoning faculty in the search after truth, thirty centuries after his age, might be justifiable; but . . . they require . . . careful scrutiny.

As a result of his scrutiny, it became clear to him that:

> Moses is not responsible for nine tenths of the Pentateuch; certainly not for the legends which have been made the bugbears of science.[2]

For Huxley this meant that the religion built on these chapters was false, and that 'refusal of assent, with willingness to re-open the question on cause shown' which was the way he defined agnosticism, was the only reasonable course. In a very similar way, many today maintain an open agnosticism, rather than commit themselves to a creed which contains so much that is incredible or superstitious; a creed which still speaks in the language of a past age. It will be my contention that a creed proclaimed in terms which directly contradict scientific understanding, can and should be rejected, but that it is open to Christians to recognise the true nature of their faith, and the way in which it demands fresh proclamation in every generation; that their faith is not bound to credal forms, to traditional and inerrant doctrinal statements and certainly not to an inerrant scripture, but that they can face the logical implications of contemporary knowledge, and still rephrase their proclamation, positively and relevantly. I shall hope to show that science drives us to take sides in the current debate, within the church, about God and about authority. To do this I shall first look briefly at the history of the relationship between science and religion; then try to isolate the real difficulties arising out of their confrontation; look at some of the solutions which have been offered; indicate how I believe the two should be seen to inter-act; and finally glance at the implications of what has been said, in the field of doctrine and a contemporary ethical problem.

Although the tension is generally associated with the figure of Darwin, it did not, historically speaking, find its origin in his publication of the *Origin of Species* in 1859. It is better to think of him as at 'the waist of an hour glass', since 'he had little real knowledge or appreciation of the ancestry of his ideas—or the climate which they created'.[3] Perhaps then, we may start with Copernicus, who dared to suggest in 1543 that the earth moved round the sun. He met with tremendous criticism and Martin Luther made the famous remark—'Some fool has gone against Holy Writ', as he remembered that Joshua said, 'Sun, stand thou still upon Gibeon, and thou moon in the valley of Aijalon' (Joshua 10[12]). If Joshua commanded sun and moon to stand still, then they must normally move. By all accounts Copernicus was talking rubbish. Galileo took the issue a stage further. A disciple of Copernicus, he was able, with the aid of a telescope, to demonstrate the copernician system, by observing Jupiter and her satellites. Many notable people refused to look, rather than see the evidence which shattered their familiar world order. From this point on, the drama unfolds with an inevitability. When Galileo went to Rome to educate the authorities, he was made to swear, in the name of catholic truth, that the earth was stationary. Today we can smile, but then, as I have earlier suggested, not only biblical authority, but the whole world order which saw man at the very centre of creation, was threatened by such an idea. Yet, even if the reaction was understandable, it is clear that the church looms large as the stifler of truth, and as circumscribing the advance of knowledge. Worse was to come.

At the beginning of the last century, the findings of the geologist posed a similar threat. Those who delighted in the literal truth of the biblical text, had, early in the 17th century, arrived at the conclusion, by studying the genealogies of Genesis, that the world was created in 4004 B.C. One can imagine their dismay when geologists began to speak of enormous periods of time, and to suggest that fossils evidenced colonisation of the land millions of years before they said Adam and Eve stood in the garden of Eden. The church's reaction was to speak of *Catastrophism*. Catastrophes were divinely engineered, and terminated earlier creations, often leaving fossils on mountain tops, if God had not placed them there specially, as others dared to suggest! The flood of the Bible was the last of these great catastrophes, and so the creation narrative of Genesis simply referred to the process following this final misfortune. In 1830 however, Lyell published his theory of *Uniformitarianism*, showing the continuous nature of the earth's history; that former changes in the earth's surface had resulted from the same forces as now operated. This put an end to the idea of a series of catastrophes. In response, the church proclaimed that the days of Genesis were symbolic of long periods of time, and that God, the creator, had acted specially at every point to create the plants and animals, as the scriptures suggested; the doctrine familiarly known as SPECIAL CREATION. Thus far, the church sought, moderately successfully, to accommodate the advance of science, and she could argue, as did a certain Christopher Benson in 1861 that 'the geologist need have no dread of interfering with the declarations of holy writ whilst pursuing his investigations into our globe's original structure and successive modifications.'[4] The world order was maintained intact, as was the Bible. However the superficiality of this judgment was to be revealed by the findings of Charles Darwin.

The hypothesis of evolution put an end to the church's doctrine of special creation, by suggesting that the various forms of life had arisen by the action of natural selection on chance variations, which arose in the course of reproduction. Darwin postulated that since there was a struggle for survival, and variations arose in offspring, those which were better adapted would survive; the principle of *survival of the fittest*. This naturally led to the idea that a gradual change, as selection acted on chance mutations, had led to the production of new forms. All this, of course, contradicted the idea of special creation, and so the church had to resort, if she wished to maintain her authority, to a *God of the gaps*. The hypothesis, it was

[51]

pointed out, was far from proven, and many steps could not be demonstrated. Where there was doubt and *no* evidence, God must have interfered to achieve his ends; a doctrine of the *God of the gaps*. The weakness of this position is obvious; as the gaps are filled in, so the image of God dwindles. Once again, the church is concerned simply to maintain doctrinal and scriptural authority.

However there was no question of the church suppressing the conclusions of Darwin, indeed his book sold 16,000 copies in its first 20 years, a remarkable achievement for a scientific publication, in those days. The strange thing was that it did not engender more reaction, and that it was an ill-conceived debate which captured the public imagination, and kept the discussion on a superficial level. A number of churchmen were clearly ready to accept the Darwinian hypothesis, even if they did not realise its implications—others were not. One of the latter party was Bishop Wilberforce and in 1860 a debate was staged between T. H. Huxley and the Bishop, who made the variously reported classic remark. . . .

> If anyone were willing to trace his descent through an ape as his grandfather, would he be willing to trace his descent similarly on the side of his grandmother?

His attempt to arouse enthusiasm to the conservative side by an appeal to Victorian horror at such degrading of the fair sex, brought forth the pointed reply from Huxley:

> I would rather have a monkey for a grandfather, than one who used great gifts to stifle the truth.

Although it would be unfair to characterise the church as simply 'head in sand', yet the debate got off to, and continued on, a very superficial level. The church's preoccupation with doctrinal and biblical authority, which is evidenced by the very great attention given to *Essays and Reviews*, compared to that given to the *Origin of Species*, meant that the real issues raised by evolutionary theory were avoided by the church's apologists. Indeed John Kent is surely right when he points out that:

> one may conclude not only that most theologians before 1914 had still not come to terms with a scientific, as distinct from a purely speculative, doctrine of evolution but that 50 years later it was still possible to ask the question, 'Have modern theologians accepted the doctrine of evolution at all?'[5]

It is not possible to give all the evidence for such a statement here, but if the logical implications of Darwinism are realised and used to evaluate the various syntheses between science and religion, which have been suggested, it is seen to be a pertinent statement.

> The problem facing the church was this, how could they protect what they took to be the core of the classical doctrine of man, while at the same time allowing for the weight of evidence which Darwin and later biologists accumulated in favour of their hypothesis.[6]

To put this another way—the Christian proclamation is based, as we have seen, on a particular doctrine of man, which in turn finds its origin in the biblical accounts of creation. Darwinism—that is to say not only evolutionary theory but just as importantly, all the geological advances before the Origin, and all that has flowed from it, saw man as a great ape trying to make good, rather than as a fallen angel, but also contribed to undermine the authority of the biblical narrative which was the basis of the church's account. It was the latter point, which most roused the Christian apologist, the implications of the former were neglected.

We may perhaps at this stage take a summary look at some of the issues raised by evolutionary theory. First, is God in control? Evolutionary theory suggests that new forms arise through the action of natural selection on chance variations; that chance rather than plan has led to the present state of the world. Is it not also arrogance to suggest that man is the peak of creation? He may one day be as extinct as the dinosaurs. Even to speak of man as the high-point of creation implies a progressionism which ill-accords with the haphazard process, which the scientist has revealed. We might further ask, at what point did man become *man*, the creature able to enter into relationship with a loving creator? Where for that matter did he get the soul, about which Christians delight to talk? The church's doctrine of man and doctrine of God are brought into question, but so too is the whole subject of atonement. Christians say that men are in a fallen state, in a state of sin and corruption. Yet evolutionary theory points to a rise from a lower to a higher form, rather than a fall from original righteousness. How then can the church speak of *re*conciliation? There never was a state of perfect bliss. Further, can she speak of the world as dis-ordered? It is, as it has always been, and human nature shares many of the characteristics of animal nature. Why, then should a man feel guilty for being the product of the interaction of his genetic inheritance and his environment? Surely sin and repentance are meaningless in

[53]

a society which is normally moral for its own good, and questions the culpability, even of inveterate criminals, as it learns more of the mechanism of development. And so one could go on, for the scientist naturally wonders at the easy acceptance of miracle, of virgin birth, and the tortuous arguments that are put forward to explain how Christ was both human and divine. Questions such as these were avoided by Christian apologists from the time of Darwin onwards, and their concern was with maintaining the authority of the biblical record, and the doctrine of God as creator and sustainer. Their lines of defence can be broadly classified under three headings.

First the HARMONISTS: basing their case on a fundamental approach to scripture.

There is the possibility of maintaining biblical authority by accepting a doctrine of plenary inspiration; that is the literal inspiration of every word, which is thus inerrant, and then producing schemes which show the actual harmony between the biblical record and scientific knowledge. These attempts to maintain biblical authority by positing plenary inspiration are found throughout the last 100 years. As late as 1932, a highly qualified professor of surgery saw fit to write:

the first chapter of Genesis is so accurate in detail that it could never have been produced by the unaided intelligence of an author, who had no more science than was known by men of his age.

In other words, here as elsewhere in holy writ:

men spake from God as they were moved by the Holy Ghost.[7]

I treasure also, a pamphlet by a colleague, which aims to prove that Moses was the author of the Pentateuch, which is of course, important if plenary inspiration of the scriptures is to be held. We may smile—or not—but I believe it to be true, that if not taking a positive fundamentalist view of the scriptures, the majority retain, what one might term a position of negative fundamentalism towards the words of the bible, treating them as literally true without realising it. This is one way then, to hold that the holy bible is inerrant, and try to show that all which the scientist says accords with it.

Then one could speak broadly of the SYNTHESISTS: going one stage further and maintaining biblical authority by reinterpreting the quality of biblical statements. At the time of Darwin, the inerrancy of scripture was not universally held, although it was certainly dominant. Its authority was maintained however, by reinterpretation.

Thus S. R. Driver, an eminent O.T. scholar of the late 19th century wrote:

> The efforts of the harmonist are praiseworthy and well meaning, but they have resulted only in the construction of artificial schemes, the unreality of which is at once detected by the scientific mind—and creates a prejudice against the entire system, with which the cosmogony is connected.

So he goes on to suggest that we should distinguish between what can and what cannot be claimed for the biblical text, and show:

> that its office is neither to anticipate scientific discovery, nor to define the lines of scientific research. It neither comes into collision with science, nor needs reconciliation with it; its office lies in a different plane altogether; it is to present ... a truthful representative picture of the relationship of God to the world.[8]

The basic idea of the authority of scripture is thus maintained, and the details of the text become of less account. This reinterpretation of biblical authority has enabled the majority of attempts at 'synthesis' between science and religion, by which, broadly speaking, the scientist has been acknowledged to reveal HOW and the theologian, through the Bible, WHY.

Although the authority of the Bible, and so the credibility of the christian proclamation may be maintained in this way, the *implications* of the theological or biblical statement have still to stand alongside scientific knowledge. When this fact is given due consideration, the majority of these syntheses are seen to be less than satisfactory to the scientist. The Christian doctrines of man and God imply a measure of *purpose* and, normally, the possibility of divine activity in the affairs of men. If these implications are unheeded, then the synthesis remains as artificial as that of the fundamentalist—and as unconvincing to the scientist. It is not possible to include a review of such syntheses here, but they seem, too often, to be pleading desperately for the scientist to recognise the possibility of God and his activity, without, apparently, recognising the weakness and illogicality of their position, and the implications which it has for faith. This is a subject to which I shall want to return, but two systems, perhaps, require and deserve more special mention. The first is that of Teilhard de Chardin.

Theologians have an ambivalent attitude to Teilhard today. Some see him as an inspired visionary, who managed to communicate Christian truth, in the terms of evolutionary thought, others find him less convincing. Briefly he reached a synthesis between science and religion, by involving Christianity in the future of the evolutionary process. A period of divergent evolution, which the scientist had described, was to be succeeded by one of convergent evolution towards what he described as the omega point. This process was to be largely in the hands of man himself, and was to be achieved through the international co-operation of mankind, promoted by the Christian gospel of love. In this way the factors which gave rise to man, and which mitigate against the purposiveness of God, are no longer judged to be extant. God is now in control, in so far as man co-operates with him to achieve his end. One can see the force of this vision, when world-government, and international co-operation, race integration and ecumenism are contemporary talking points, but does it paint too rosy a picture of the potential in man? Does it place Christian hope too far in the future for the gospel to remain present good news for a tortured humanity, and does it undermine the element of risk in faith? We shall want to return to all this.

Process theology is the other system to which reference should be made. This moves one stage further, and seeks to explain, almost demonstrate, the activity of God. It arises from the process philosophy of A. N. Whitehead, rediscovered after 40 years, sweeping America, and powerfully proclaimed by such men as Norman Pittenger, in this country. Whitehead noted the inter-relatedness of things, and their mutual influence on one another. (Evolutionary theory is obviously acceptable!) He based his philosophy on the idea of PROCESS, as an expression of this inter-relatedness. Process theology simply posits God within this mutually interacting system; able to influence, and be influenced by what happens in the world. Again, we may, I think, ask whether faith remains faith, if the activity of God is thus demonstrated, and also realise that the system demands more flexibility of the scientist than most of them would allow.

The question of scientific flexibility, leads me to glance at a third possibility—REDUCTIONISM. Some would deny that the Christian proclamation is challenged by science, either by undermining the confidence of the scientist or by reducing the claims of the Christian faith. It is possible to argue that evolutionary theory is far from proved. It was not universally accepted at the time of Darwin, has subsequently received modification, and still is incomplete. This is true, but in principal it stands the test of time, and though it is possible to point to gaps in the theory, to underline the uncertainty of the scientist, and to rejoice in the element of faith in his speculations, you merely perpetuate the God of the gaps, by so doing. Such apologists should not seriously detain us.

Those who reduce the challenge of Christian faith, must also be treated with disdain, though this approach is more difficult to define. When radical theologians can say no more than the humanist, something is radically wrong! The Christian has a gospel, and stands for an attitude to life which may be rejected, but may not be denied to be effective for himself. It must be true that what he says can stand in a positive relationship to the contribution of the scientist, without losing its potency.

So I would contend, and I have tried to hint at this as I went along, that all these attempts may help some, but are not universally satisfying, as they fail either to do justice to the scientist or to the theologian, or are simply untenable by a rational person. Nor do I imagine that the following synthesis will achieve universal acclamation, but it is reached as a result of the conviction that the questions posed by the present scientific world view must be faced squarely, and that christians rather than reinterpreting their faith and redefining traditional categories out of existence, should consider whether the time may not have come for a fresh approach. All the conclusions so far considered, result from the attempt to reach a synthesis between two distinct positions. That of the Christian, who posits God as the creator and sustainer of life, with a purpose for the world which he daily effects, and that of the scientist, who claims to be discovering the *real* nature of life and the possibilities in man. Since this inevitably leads to a clash in authority, which has been remarked upon, a way forward may be found if the doctrine of the church and the authority of its scriptures, can be redefined. This possibility is particularly pertinent in the light of two factors. The first is the reassessment of doctrine in the light of existential theology, the second, the redefinition of biblical authority as a result of contemporary critical method. Both are being debated today, the latter as strongly as it was one hundred years ago. Taking seriously the results of such an approach to doctrine and scripture may suggest an alternative method of arriving at a synthesis between science and religion. It may be better to start from *what we know* in both disciplines rather than what is 'revealed', and see whether this is contradictory, or whether the two can mutually illuminate one another. This is possible when we

E

approach faith and its communication from the standpoint of the existential theologian.

The existentialist is, above all, the prophet of self-awareness and the existential theologian warns the Christian not to try to impose God on people—that is a God who is defined as almighty, creator, love, judge etc. Instead we are to ask people about their existence—its nature and its needs. His aim is to lead them to a straight choice—not between a God, defined as active in a way which the scientist finds incredible, and no God; but between self-sufficiency and dependence, between self-interest and responsibility. Any man may be asked—when you examine your own life, are you confident in your ability to direct it—to achieve balance and purpose—or do you long for a purpose to which you can become obedient—a meaning which will give you direction? No such meaning and purpose are written into life—other than 'survival of the fittest'—and the decision to live according to such a pattern is therefore an act of faith, which is found to open up new creative possibilities, and miraculously, to transform human nature itself. Responsibility in life, for life, is acknowledged to be ultimate, rather than a matter of personal choice, and this is communicated as 'belief in God', and as obedience to his will. Christian belief is thus an interpretation of my existence, and it frees me from the menace of the world, not by denying it, or looking for Utopia and future reward, but, potentially by transforming the here and now. This is good news!

Strangely enough, it is possible today, to say that this is no more than the earliest writer of Genesis (J) was claiming. Critical method, which results in a reappraisal of biblical inspiration and authority, makes it possible to suggest that the Jahwist was not concerned to *reveal the truth* about the origin of man, but to describe man as he saw him with the eyes of faith. The story of the disobedience of Adam and Eve is not a historical description, nor does it explain the fallen state of man—it does describe the present nature of man, who, born for dependence and responsibility has an inherent tendency to imagine that he knows better than God, and to reject him. This leads to an ever-increasing circle of sin, where sin is the disruption of the harmony of creation. If this is correct, both as an interpretation of the aim of the Jahwist, and of the nature of man, then, this early writer saw, as clearly as we do today, the challenge facing man in every generation, and it is as vital to realise this positive possibility in the words of scripture, as it is to realise the implications of scientific advance. Proclaiming Christianity is not a process of proclaiming the incredible against all reason, nor is it to proclaim humanism. It is to suggest the possibility of transforming human nature, by accepting the meaningless as *meaningful*, the purposeless as *purposeful*— a possibility open to all men, the scientist included, if there can be humility and a capacity to respond.

This basic challenge accepted, its rationalisation and communication demand that we formulate doctrine, but this must be doctrine which is in harmony with the age in which we live. This is not to claim too high a place for science, it is simply to state that Christian communication has to reflect contemporary culture. The categories of a pre-scientific age *may* not be adequate to communicate faith in the 20th century. On the contrary this century should *expect* to reinterpret the faith in communication as has constantly been done before. (e.g. As can be seen when the theological standpoints of J, D, P and the Chronicler and Apocalyptist are compared. They share the same basic faith, but communicate it in the cultural terms of their own time.) It is not possible in a paper of this length to examine, in detail, the implications of this approach, but I want to go on to look briefly at some areas in which I believe, Christians will have to be prepared to exercise the utmost flexibility, if the gospel is to make any impact, remembering that we do this from the standpoint of our faith, which, as I have suggested, cannot be assaulted by the advance of knowledge.

The Christian will first want to recognise *the quality of the language* which he uses. Christianity is, basically, a personal experience; it is what I make of my life, and it cannot, therefore, be communicated as objective fact. Its communication is akin to the attempt of the artist or the poet to communicate, rather than the historian or reporter. This suggests that the language used is *mythological*, where this term is not equivalent to fairy-tale, but is used to include all imagery and language used to communicate personal experience. One brief example: the three-decker universe so despised as pre-scientific, can also be treated as positive mythology, in the sense in which it reflects and communicates human experience. In so far as it is broadly true that life runs in three planes (moments of exaltation, depression and the normal level of existence) it can be said to express more than an early understanding of the universe. So just as the Jahwist takes over traditional material, and employs it to communicate his insight into the nature of faith and humanity, we ought to ask, what sort of 'myths' we should employ today.

For example, when considering the *Doctrine of God*, our study may suggest that it is inadvisable to start from a prior affirmation of God, as creator and sustainer of the Universe. The connotation of these words, the common misunderstanding of the quality of language, and the implications of taking the existentialist position, all combine to suggest that this will be a stumbling-block to the outsider and, significantly, fail to express best our own experience. One would rather say that faith in the purposiveness of life, that is in the dependent, creative role of man, is best expressed by speaking about God. If further definition is needed, then perhaps the phrase of Tillich that describes God as 'The ground of being' is liable to cause the least confusion. Similarly, when the *doctrine of Christ* is discussed, it may be that we shall not want to start from the emphatic assertion of the two natures, human and divine, in the one person, with its imponderable associations. Instead, if the traditional categories used to express his uniqueness, both of person and activity, have lost some of their power, Christians must feel free to search for redefinition. Virgin-birth may make sense to the faithful, it fails to convince the scientist of the uniqueness of Christ. Rather, we may want to start from our solid position of faith and its possibilities, and say that here, in a unique and challenging way, the Christian possibility is enshrined. His death is an unavoidable challenge to find meaning in life, and the resurrection, the result of this possibility.

If we go on to consider the *doctrine of the spirit*, it may be that we shall want no longer to say that the spirit is given or received in baptism, confirmation or at any other time, but rather that the Holy Spirit expresses the empowering which we experience through our relationship with God. Since this experience is personal, intangible even fleeting, *sacraments* are a necessary corollary. Not in order that the Christian may receive grace or the spirit, in the sense in which these are quantitative, to be stored and treasured, but in the sense that his awareness of the relationship, on which his life is based, may be intensified and kept alive.

These are no more than brief indications of the sort of flexibility I would judge to be necessary in the formulation of doctrine, and the communication of the Christian faith. The necessity arises, when the logical implications of scientific advance are taken seriously by the man of faith. This suggests that the Christian may not treat as peripheral the current debate within the church, on all aspects of doctrine and belief. However, it is not to suggest that all that is traditional is to be jettisoned, but rather that we must all entertain the possibility that he who would communicate the faith will need to employ new images and myths, if these best suit his purpose. For some a straight proclamation of sin forgiven, may still have power and be good news, for others it may be meaningless. The disciple must be free and willing to look for new categories, which can excite the outsider and still be true to the faith, which he experiences, if he is to challenge the world.

And challenge we must, because in the last analysis, the most significant factor which arises from allowing scientific advance to structure and influence your theology, and follows from the re-appraisal we have made of faith and its communication, is that *the individual matters*. The Christian gospel is not just about life after death, pie in the sky and the golden age to come, it is as Jesus patently showed, good news now. While the whole tenor of evolutionary theory suggests that the individual is of little account, and the weak are to be despised; the Christian, who acknowledges the purpose in the world, must believe in equality of purpose, and therefore of opportunity for all men. This is indeed good news. A proper attention to scientific advance may have freed Christian proclamation from outworn traditional categories, in an exhilarating way, it also isolates and underlines the real challenge with which the Christian faces the scientist and, indeed, all men—the worth of the individual.

There are finally, some further implications of this study in the field, which one might broadly term, eugenics. Historically, the church could be accused of preventing or hampering the advance of knowledge, but clearly, scientific advance is inevitable and should be welcomed by Christians, provided that they are equally aware of their contribution. So one may suggest that taking Darwinism seriously involves the possibility of a complete re-appraisal of Christian proclamation, a process which is enabled by existential theology and critical method. The proper use of these tools leaves science and religion, each making their contribution to man's self-awareness, but also isolates the real tension between them. This is a tension caused not by the question of God and his activity, nor even by the Christian's arrogant assumptions about man's place in creation, but by his insight into the possibilities inherent in his own life. When the Christian affirms purposiveness in life, and speaks of his 'ultimate responsibility' towards others, he directly contradicts his own nature, which the scientist sees, and indeed the Jahwist saw, is more nearly akin to 'every man for himself'—at least when put to the test. This may involve the Christian in the posibility of once more seeking to restrict the scientist in the future. Let me put it this way. The suffering of man, war, hunger, racial tension etc., all make talk of 'Utopia' inevitable. The question is, is this a real hope or illusory, and how will it be achieved? Jews and Christians have stated in the past, that it will come through *the power of God*. God will one day act to vindicate his chosen people. This has not happened and it may reasonably be asked, whether it ever will. The alternative is to look for its achievement through *the power of man*. If this involves as it surely must, the willing co-operation of man, there is a bleak outlook, but what if it should be possible through force?

It is significant that in 1969, man is on the threshold of obtaining the potential power to achieve Utopia. His understanding of the processes of life and development have reached such a stage that the ability to mould the future is predictably realisable. The key to this lies in the understanding and so potential control of his own environment, and the understanding and control of reproduction, and even length of life. Animal husbandry has been largely responsible for the majority of advances in reproductive techniques, and this will continue to be the case. The demands of the world for food, mean that, for example, fecundity, sex-selection, sperm storage and artificial insemination are all extremely advantageous to the farmer. They allow him the possibility of producing unlimited animals of the right sex and pedigree, long after the death of a particular animal. Even more exciting to the farmer would be the possibility raised by contemporary advances in genetic engineering and selective breeding and the prospect opened up by the technique of 'cloning'. These would enable the production of any number of identical offspring, with selected characteristics, if it should prove possible to develop the technique of vitriparity (the rearing of embryos in what is familiarly called a 'test-tube').

As a result, the techniques of husbandry would become almost unrecognisable. Yet these techniques, some already perfected, some in the experimental stage, others predicted and all, surely, within the realms of possibility, could very well become possibilities for man also. Further, in the face of over-population, there could well be a desire to limit reproduction, and then the attraction of these techniques becomes obvious. Many of them involve difficulties, not just ethically, but medically, since they require surgery, but they are still insidiously attractive to a society which enjoys its freedom and outstrips its food supply. It does not seem fanciful to suggest that society could deem control of the reproduction of the species desirable. One has only to think of the current pressures on Indians to limit their families, and of the less moderate attitude of the Chinese to malformation. Already in this country, diabetes and other conditions have been recognised as genetic defects, and advances have been made in detecting malformation in utero. More recently a link has been forged between a psychopathic state and the presence of YY chromosomes. Such advances raise the whole question of who should reproduce, and which pregnancies should be terminated, for the good of society and the future. Equally poignant problems are raised by transplant techniques at the other end of the life span.

Utopia then, it would appear, is a real possibility, if we could determine what blue print would, in fact, benefit mankind which is far from clear. What is clearer, is that the possibilities for unscrupulous exploitation are immense, and in the face of the economic and social pressures which the next decades will bring, attractive. An awareness of the findings of the scientist, should prompt the Christian to ask what stand, if any, he can take on these important issues. He may not attempt to circumscribe the advance of the scientist, but his role could yet appear restrictive, should he decide for example, that he must maintain the inalienable right of the individual over against society. At the very least, he will surely want to say that the individual has the right of freedom of choice, when the issues affecting the future of man are made clear. Utopia, for the Christian, is not a future golden age, heavenly or earthly, certainly not if this is gained at the expense of the individual.

So then, a proper respect for the advance of knowledge, a positive evaluation of critical method and existential theology and the consequent redefinition both of proclamation and communication of the faith, will lead the Christian to a firm position from which to make his unique contribution to man's self-awareness. This positive process is a necessary prerequisite to defining his stand on the many ethical problems, which face him now and in the foreseeable future.

References:

1. T. H. Huxley, *Science and Christian Tradition.*
2. Ibid.
3. Himmelfarb, *Darwin and the Darwinian Revolution.*
4. C. Benson, *First and second verses of the Book of Genesis examined,* 1861.
5. John Kent, *From Darwin to Blatchford.*
6. Ibid.
7. Rendle Short, *Bible in Modern Research.*
8. Article in *The Expositor,* 1886.

To Love God with the Mind

Geoffrey Paul

A sermon in the middle of the conference; and a sermon by a non-philosopher and a non-scientist. I found myself asking what its function was. Well, clearly it is not its function to read one more paper, and it's not its function to anticipate the final lecture. In this context of prayer, its function, it seems to me, is to ensure that this conference on issues in religion and science shall not only be an intellectual exercise, but shall also be worship.

And so I take what seems the obvious text: You shall love the Lord your God with all your mind. This is part of Jesus' reply in Mark xii. 30 to the scribe who asked what was the great commandment of the law.

Now it would be nice to draw attention to the fact that the words 'with all your mind' do not occur in the Hebrew text and so are not found in our English text of Deuteronomy, which has only 'with all your heart and with all your soul and with all your strength', and maintain that the command to love God with your mind is a specifically Christian insight, in fact that it was an interpretation of the meaning of the Old Testament command made by Jesus himself. But it's not quite so straightforward as that. In the first place, the words 'with all your mind' *do* occur in the more generally accepted texts of the Septuagint, and of course the Hebrew word 'heart' includes the powers of the mind. What is more, it would be a bold man who would *insist* that the four Greek words correspond with four Aramaic words Jesus must have spoken on this occasion: the order of words varies in the parallel passages, and in one passage it isn't Jesus who speaks them, and there would in any case be some likelihood of the text approximating to the text of the Septuagint, which was more commonly used in the early church than the Hebrew text. But the fact that the words 'with all your mind' do occur in both the parallel passages, and the fact that both Jesus and the apostles after him do insist on the functions of the mind in Christian devotion make me think that those who wrote down the words 'with all your mind' believed that they had rightly understood Jesus' intention, and that the mind therefore *has* a function in our love for God.

So I think then that it is fair to ask, What is implied in this Christian command, You shall love the Lord your God with all your mind?

Well, first it is worth stopping to consider for a moment man's rational faculty, the mind, as an instrument of religious devotion. And plainly the context, You shall *love* the Lord your God with all your mind means that we are not here concerned with the use of the mind to clear away difficulties or overcome doubts *before* belief: we are concerned with the use of the mind in the context of faith, of love, of dedication, of the worship of a God already accepted as the Lord your God.

Christians haven't always been too happy to give the mind an equal position along with the heart and the soul in their devotion. And make no mistake about it, there are plenty of forces ranged against the mind today.

It has been common enough to fear that the mind was more likely to disturb faith; it has been common enough to decry the mind as representing man's own proud self-sufficiency, his temptation to imagine he can find out and arrange everything for himself without humble dependence on God. I had plenty of friends as a student who used to shake their heads and say, 'Trust in the Lord with all thine heart, and lean not to thine own understanding'. I used to pooh-pooh what seemed to me an obscurantist use of that text from Proverbs, but after living alongside illiterate Christians, I know that often simple unthinking souls will have acted boldly in unreflecting trust while their more learned brothers are still sitting on the fence debating. And I remember that fine intellect Emile Cammaerts once lamenting how much harder the power of the mind made faith and saying, 'But I hope in the day of judgement God will make some allowances for us poor intellectuals'.

If you smile, you may remember that this is the burden of much existential philosophy today. The existentialists have been concerned to expose the superficiality of merely disinterested reflection and have argued that real knowing comes by decision of the will, by commitment and involvement—to use today's blessed words.

Or again, think how in the recently independent countries, or among university students, the old liberal Christian tradition seems so completely outdated—the tradition by which we prided ourselves on trying to see every side of a question. Who cares for impartiality now—today's heroes are either reactionaires or revolutionaries, either way partisans and not rationalists.

The mind comes under fire from another direction. Think of the Pentecostals—in South America the fastest growing church in the whole world. They look for a clear demonstration of the presence of the Holy Spirit in the believer in manifestations involving the emotional or subliminal instincts, in phenomena over which the mind and reason have little control.

It is a sobering thought that now when for the first time in history we have universal education, respect for the mind is at a discount. The intellectual is written off along with the colonialist, the middle classes, the armchair observer. And anyone who argues, as I am arguing here, that the mind has a proper function in religious devotion may thereby merely be bringing religious devotion into contempt. For many people today there is more immediate appeal in the name LSD than in the phrase 'your reasonable worship'— whatever it means.

Against all these attacks on reason, we ought unequivocally to maintain that reason, the rational faculties, the mind, are the chief distinctive faculty of man, what distinguishes us from the animals, as emotion and instinct do not. And therefore it is of the highest importance to insist and to go on insisting that the mind should have a proper place in man's devotion to God.

It is, of course, because the mind in the liberal rationalist tradition has been isolated and exalted above the other faculties that it has come under such heavy fire of late. And that leads on to the second point arising from my text. The mind is set in the context of heart, soul and strength, and the command is the strange one 'to *love* with the mind'.

How do you do that? What is loving with the mind? Well, clearly it is more than impartial reflection. One thinks of the dedicated, passionate use of the mind that distinguishes the scientist following out a hypothesis, tracking down evidence needs to confirm some bit of inspired guess-work, trying through night after night of calculations to make a coherent picture from apparently intractable observations. It is not hard to see how a scientist loves with his mind.

But how does a Christian love with his mind when we are thinking of his devotion to God?

First of all, our imagination is part of our mind, and we do use our imagination in trying to please our wives or our girl-friends. Is there a use of the imagination in our devotion to God? At present a great deal of imagination goes into the production of ad hoc services, but often I suspect, it is devoted to securing the maximum participation on the part of the congregation. I wonder if that is really the same as using our imagination in aiming to please God for himself. This is not an easy idea to follow up, as obviously we can't surprise God, as we try to surprise our wives with unexpected presents, and again some attempts in the past to please God by imaginative acts have been fussy and trivial. But perhaps to love God with the imagination does mean to discover ways of reverence that are natural to us in this generation.

Again, to love with the mind means simply to allow love to take hold of one more level of our personality. Many people begin to love with the affections, and then measure their love by their feelings. The traditional catholic teaching on prayer was that prayer gradually moved from vocal prayer, the natural expression of religious feeling, to discursive meditation, when one's mind began to nourish itself on the Bible, and so worship to God as He more truly is, rather than God as made solely in the image of one's experience. St. Paul says essentially the same thing when he writes, 'And I pray that your love may abound yet more and more in knowledge and all discernment', so that you may distinguish the more important from the less important. 'To love with the mind' is a description of Christian maturity whereby our love for God refines and matures our judgement. I remember being impressed by the opinion of a fairly critical observer that the Revival Movement in East Africa had begun to produce Christian thinking at levels hardly envisaged before. St Paul again emphasises that the break with worldliness comes as Christians undergo the 'renewing of your mind', and that this is part of the offering of ourselves in reasonable worship.

And then classically, men have loved God with the mind—with more or less effect—by writing volumes of theology. Here is the attempt to set forth or to defend the honour of God to oneself or to others. It is the refusal to allow the object of one's devotion to remain but a series of irreconcilable vignettes or blurred images;

the desire to focus one's attention on God in his coherent beauty, to prepare in part for the vision of God. It is the attempt to paint such a consistent picture to others that they will be attracted to God.

And this leads on to the complete phrase of my text, 'You shall love the Lord your God with all your mind', for I think this is in essence a command to each one of us in his way to be a dedicated and willing theologian, a command to each of us to pray, to think, to act and to react theologically, until the refined and renewed mind has controlled and directed all the faculties in the direction of God, and the understanding of God has been immeasurably enlarged.

It is a marvellous thing to watch how this happened in the case of someone like St. Paul.

He first came to know and love Christ not intellectually, but in an overwhelming experience of rebuke and forgiveness that came to him through his only semi-rational faculties, and that had at the time direct and uncontrollable physical effects upon him. But he goes on allowing this experience to penetrate and fill his mind. He reflects upon his experience, testing it both against scripture and against the situations into which he carries the gospel. And by this means theology and the knowledge and indeed the glory of God are enhanced for all men.

He reflects on his experience of Christ as justifier; on Christ's power to give new meaning to the whole of the Jewish tradition behind him; on Christ's authoritative bearing and his power over nature; or his conviction of being sent, and of bearing the whole of God's will and purpose in himself. And when Paul is faced with the suggestion that there are other powers, particularly the powers of fate with which a man has to reckon in life, we find him matching all that experience and reflection to this challenge, and the result is the marvellous words.

He is the image of the unseen God, the mould and pattern of all creation; for in him were all things created both in heaven and on earth, seen and unseen, by whatever names these mighty and fearful powers are called; all things were created by him and for him. He is before all things and all things find their significance and coherence in him.

This is theology sung aloud in praise.

It is an enlargement of the understanding of Christ over anything that had gone before.

It is an expression of the love of Paul's whole mind for God.

A small footnote. Can't theologising go wrong and instead of being praise be a deforming and a distortion? Well, on the one hand, we cannot make God greater than He is, so there is nothing to fear in pushing our experience, tested by scripture, to the limits of its meaning. But on the other hand, of course the individual can go wrong, and produce defective theology—who can't see the defects even in the marvellous edifices of St. Augustine or Teilhard de Chardin or whoever it may be. But the promise of the Holy Spirit to lead into all truth is, like all His gifts, made primarily to the church as a whole. And where in the church there is a fearless, vigorous theological life, it will be grateful for its one-sided giants, and will, perhaps slowly, be able to absorb their insights into a larger rounded whole.

To love God with all your mind means to give your experience of God the fullest weight in your thinking, to test it against scripture, tradition and the corporate mind of the church, and then to put it against the challenges and puzzles and problems each generation produces, and to find ourselves praising God that He is only seen bigger and more glorious in each new context.

If the true scientists see that there is a glad, fearless, confident yet humble use for the mind in the love of God, they will, I believe, listen when theologians declare that the mind is not the only means of reaching truth or of serving God.

Seminar Group Reports—
A Summary

1. 'I am convinced that there is no more substantial nourishment for the religious life than contact with scientific realities, properly understood.' How far is this attitude of Teilhard de Chardin acceptable to the contemporary church?

   There are quite a number of concepts that require definition— 'substantial nourishment', 'religious life' and 'scientific reality'. Our answer depends ultimately on what we mean by these terms. We did feel, however, that scientific reality was an important constituent of religious life, in this particular historic period of human culture, but that fundamentally prayer, worship and personal contact with God remains more important than a contact with scientific reality, however defined.

2. Karl Popper has suggested a Hippocratic oath for scientists. Can an ethical system really be derived from science?

   It was decided that we must first produce a working definition of science if we are to answer this question. The definition which we produced was that science is the attempt to find out *what is*, as opposed to a code of ethics which is concerned with *what ought to be*. If we accept this then no code of ethics can be derived from science. Nevertheless ethical systems are derived from different world views in which science may play a greater or lesser part. If science consciously were to orient itself to the betterment of man rather than solely to the betterment of knowledge, then an ethical system might well be derived from it.

[70]

3. Is a 'dialogue' between contemporary science and religion a genuine possibility?

Perhaps the question would have been better posed as 'is a dialogue possible between scientists and men of religion' rather than between science and religion? However, both science and religion share similar origins. The quest is obviously one for meaning. The scientist is looking for some sort of meaning and order and that, of course, is also what concerns the man of religion. In terms of individual psychology many scientists who are religious carry on some sort of dialogue within themselves whereby they make a kind of reconciliation. Also it was noted of course, that many of the leading physicists of the 20th century have of necessity become philosophers. Physics has disappeared into philosophy and hence only one step away from religion. Further, dialogue between men can be set off at least by mutual respect for our commitment and intellectual honesty. Respect for a man for his intellectual stature in itself is obviously a catalyst to any sort of dialogue.

The popular image of science as being something which could answer everything if it was only given the time and opportunity, had created an attitude, in which discussion had been found to be difficult. Dialogue was now encouraged by two major changes; on the side of science by the acceptance of relativity, the question of objectivity and subjectivity, the new approach to scientific method; on the side of religion by the felt need to be open to scrutiny by the methodology of science, an attitude which is comparatively recent.

4. Does the future of theology lie in the interdisciplinary studies with the sciences? With which of the sciences in particular?

After the Darwinian controversy, theology retreated into its own field and it was agreed that academic theology can continue in a very restricted field without any real reference to science. If theology however, is to be relevant to the whole of life and if it is to be 'open ended', then its future must be inter-disciplinary with all subjects. Even academic theology might learn something from the methodology of the sciences. But it must not solely be an interdisciplinary approach with the sciences, the traditional arts had a significant contribution to make to any discussion of the human situation. The social sciences also had an important relevance, particularly to pastoral theology.

[71]

5. Are the 'models of science' and the 'analogues of faith' mutually excluding or complementary?

Discussion was concerned particularly with the function of the major 'analogues of faith', in particular truth, law, pattern, end and purpose and order, as well as specific concepts like atonement. We noted that both scientific models and analogues of faith seem to have a provisional quality about them. We felt that there must be a universe rather than a multiverse, and that truth ultimately is one. The models of science and 'analogues of faith' must be complementary not self-excluding.